'With enviable powers of recall, [Carol Dyhouse] takes us through a moving account of the changing personal significance of clothes as she grows up and moves into later life. Part personal memoir and part brilliantly researched social history, this study of women's engagement with appearance, and the commercial imperatives that feed it, will be compelling for readers of all ages.'

MARCIA POINTON, PROFESSOR EMERITA IN
HISTORY OF ART, UNIVERSITY OF MANCHESTER

'In this intimate journey through clothes, perfume and make-up, Dyhouse shows us exactly why appearance matters to women. It is a wonderful read – by turns funny and poignant – packed with acute observation, entertaining anecdote and wonderful historical detail.'

PROFESSOR CLAIRE LANGHAMER,
DIRECTOR OF THE INSTITUTE OF HISTORICAL RESEARCH

'A memoir told through clothes, this book not only charts the author's life but the cultural and societal shifts in post-war Britain. Both a trip down memory lane and an entertaining slice of fashion history.'

KATIE GODMAN, FASHION HISTORIAN
AND AUTHOR OF *GOTHIC FASHION – THE HISTORY*

'Dyhouse skillfully combines autobiography and biography in a history of women and girls' ambiguous relationship with their appearance. Wide-ranging research underpins a scholarly, witty, profound book speaking to, and of, a generation of women experiencing new educational and employment opportunities.'

STEPHANIE SPENCER,
EMERITA PROFESSOR, UNIVERSITY OF WINCHESTER

Appearances

Appearances

MEMORY · HISTORY · CLOTHES

CAROL DYHOUSE

UNICORN

Contents

ONE	Coming Apart at the Seams: My Life in Clothes	7
TWO	Crinoline Ladies	36
THREE	School Uniforms	46
FOUR	Sex Kitten, Beat Girl	59
FIVE	Baby Dolls and Dollybirds	66
SIX	Classy Looks	76
SEVEN	Power Dressing	85
EIGHT	Dress and Defiance	94
NINE	Mail Order, Mirrors and Murmurations	103
TEN	Glamour and Feminism	109
ELEVEN	Scent Trails	117
TWELVE	Adornment: Glitter, Poppets and Pearls	129
THIRTEEN	Adornment: Make-up	138
FOURTEEN	My Mother's Clothes, and her Mother's	148
FIFTEEN	Daughters: Memories, Threads	157
SIXTEEN	Dress and Desire	175
SEVENTEEN	History through Clothes	182
EIGHTEEN	Sorting, Clearing, Letting Go	190

References 198
Acknowledgements 208
Picture Credits 209
Index 210

ONE

Coming Apart at the Seams: My Life in Clothes

I'M OF AN AGE when people look back over their lives, trying to draw threads together, looking for patterns. They go about this in all manner of ways. Writers such as Jane Miller or Diana Athill have in recent years explored the experience of reaching old age in literary memoir, weaving in memories of youth and maturity. Others look for order in more practical tasks; they sort possessions and clear out drawers. My mother, unwell and nearing the end of her life, attacked a huge collection of family photographs, sorting them into fat albums, one for each of her four children.

How do you select from memory in striving to piece together narratives and thus make sense of a life? It must depend, in part, on temperament and values, as well as on gender and an awareness of cultural norms. Men have traditionally chronicled careers and life in the public sphere, often saying very little about their loves, wives and families; women's stories tend to turn the focus around, and have historically been more fragmented, familial and private. Women's recall of the past can be shot through with images of clothing, and what they were wearing at particular moments in their lives. Such memories often provoke strong feelings, whether of pleasure or pain.

In 1925, Virginia Woolf, regularly tormented over appearances, made a note in her diary resolving to write about clothes, adding 'My love of clothes interests me profoundly: only it is not love; & what it is I must discover.' She was then in her forties, and well established as a writer. Almost a century later, Claire Wilcox, Senior Curator of Fashion at the V&A, published a wonderfully dreamlike and poetic memoir entitled *Patch Work: A Life Amongst Clothes*. It is essentially a series of meditations on her life, interwoven with deep knowledge about the personal and historic meanings and pleasures of clothes.

In seeking to look back on, and to make sense of, my own life, I find that I too want to write about clothes. In my case this will be less of a celebration than an attempt to understand why clothes have mattered so much, and why how to dress has always been for me a source of tension and trouble as well as delight. I want to draw threads together, certainly, but I know this will produce a puckering, a tangle, rather than an effect of smoothness. And I hope that an attempt to look dispassionately at this tangle will yield insights into more than mere personal obsessions and pathology, and that it will throw light on some of the predicaments posed and experienced by women since the Second World War.

I was born three years after the war ended: I still have a (part-used) clothing coupon ration book issued in my name from then. I don't remember thinking much about how my clothes looked on me in early childhood, although I well remember the *feel* of certain garments: a horrible 'liberty bodice' with rubber buttons; a deliciously fluffy white angora-wool bolero. There was also an angora hat that I loved because it was studded with little silver and pink stars. When I think about what I wore as a child I am mostly dependent on photographs, rather than being able to retrieve images from my own memory. An exception were the outfits my mother planned for my brother and me to celebrate the Coronation. Mum had run up special costumes for us in crepe paper: red, white and blue. She stuck little gold crowns on them. But alas, it looked like rain on

CHAPTER ONE

Coronation Day morning and knowing how the colour in wet crepe paper bleeds, Mum decided to forgo our special outfits. Instead, we wore our 'dressing-up' clothes. My brother had a cowboy suit, I was dressed as a tiny nurse. I wore a blue dress, covered with a white apron, a large red cross emblazoned on my infant chest. Gender messages seeped into what we did and what we wore, as unambiguous as the messages about girls and boys in the Ladybird reading books. On Saturdays, I went shopping with my mother and grandmother. My brother stayed with my father and they shut themselves away in the garage with woodwork. Dad made a doll's house for me, and a fort for my brother, using painted plywood.

Becoming a bridesmaid was a big event in my childhood. Mum and my 'Auntie' Phyl next door agonised over what to do about my lank and weedy hair. My grandmother had occasionally persuaded this into ringlets, Victorian style. But this required winding strands round and round with rags, and not being able to sleep at night with what looked and felt like stiff tentacles protruding from my head. Mum normally scraped my hair back into tight plaits, but for my uncle's wedding, she and Auntie Phyl thought they'd try a home perm. A 'Toni' home-perm kit it was, with stinky solutions and curlers that looked like plastic chicken bones. The result was a lot of frizz. I was photographed in my puff-sleeved bridesmaid's dress of primrose net, carrying a bunch of artificial primroses tied with gold and silver ribbon. I can't remember whose choices these were, but I may have had some input. The posy of primroses appealed, I remember, because it was what Maria carried at her wedding to Robin in what had become a favourite children's book of mine, Elizabeth Goudge's *The Little White Horse* (1946).

I was a voracious reader as a child, and through reading, I started to learn about clothes. Goudge's female characters, Maria and Loveday, wore dresses in fabrics which set me dreaming. Maria wore grey silk, edged with white fur and

Permed hair and primrose nylon. Me as bridesmaid, 1950s.

crystal beads. Tiny bunches of violets were tucked into her bonnet and muff. There were pelisses in velvet and gowns of pale satin, the colour of moonbeams.

My parents had a small bookcase with a shelf of Book Club edition volumes, printed on thin 'War Economy Standard' paper. Amongst these I came across Anya Seton's historical romance, *Dragonwyck*. I found this story of Miranda's fascination with the brooding gothic hero, Nicholas Van Ryn, particularly stirring. Miranda, from an austerely religious and provincial country background, hankers after romance and sophistication and finds it in New York and in the opulent feudal setting of the grand country house, Dragonwyck. Nicholas, Lord of the Manor of Dragonwyck, and her new guardian and employer, finds Miranda's simple brown Merino dress and unfashionable country bonnets 'hideous' and he orders 'Madame Duclos in New York' to kit her out with a complete trousseau of clothes, perfumes and toiletries. I drooled over the details of silk dresses, 'one green, with black velvet trimming on the flounces, one a rose evening gown festooned with blond lace' and all the accessories: kid shoes, ivory fans and beaded reticules. The descriptions of clothes were luscious. Miranda comes to learn how clothes indicate social position and cultural values, realises how untutored was her previous taste in dress. Through my reading, I learned all this, too.

By the time I graduated to junior school, I was well aware of clothes as a source of desire, delight and longing, but aware, at the same time, that since people would judge you on what you wore, you could get it badly wrong. Secondary school, with its stringent requirements around school uniform, swung a massive wrecking ball into all this, obliterating most of the delight and pleasure. The theory behind school uniform often claims that it is egalitarian: everyone looks the same. But they don't of course. Our uniform – in a selective girls' grammar in the Midlands – was expensive. Parents of new entrants were supplied with a detailed list of items to be purchased from a classy supplier. It seemed endless. Gabardine tunics, shirts and ties, summer hats, winter hats, indoor and outdoor shoes. Games kit in house colours, overalls for science. With casual racism the colour stipulated was 'Nigger Brown': at that time almost all the pupils at the school were white. Girls whose parents tried to economise might be conspicuous on account of garments sewn or knitted at home which attempted to replicate the more expensive kit bought from the official supplier. And their stuff was probably named with inked-on letters, rather than sewn with woven Cash's name tapes.

School uniform was also about hierarchy, discipline, the obliteration of individuality and the rigorous suppression of any burgeoning sexuality in adolescent girls. The gymslip-type tunics were tight across the chest and had to be worn with collar and tie. Skirt length was strictly regulated, as was the 'denier' or thickness of tights. My mother observed that as a grammar school girl in the 1930s, she had been obliged to wear black stockings: they had been unfashionable then and she had hated them. In the 1960s black stockings were much more fashionable and so the girls' schools, predictably, came to frown on them. It was the same with the length of skirts. Short in the 1930s might mean girlishly acceptable. In the 1960s it signalled sexy and was banned.

The school I attended, Solihull High School for Girls, was housed in a wonderful old building, once an elegant eighteenth-century mansion, called Malvern Hall. The headmistress was Flora Macrae Forster. She was a scholar who had studied at Somerville College, Oxford, alongside Vera Brittain and Margaret Kennedy (a close friend of hers, who after Oxford achieved fame as the author of the best-selling novel, *The Constant Nymph*). Miss Forster was what I can best describe as 'a gentlewoman'. She took a tough line on anything she considered representative of female pusillanimity, and discouraged girls' interest in fashion and appearance. For many years, even her staff were forbidden to wear lipstick; it would have been considered 'vulgar'. In the late 1950s, teenage girls loved to puff out their skirts with what were then called 'paper nylon petticoats', sometimes starched at home in sugar water. This was a particular bugbear of Miss Forster's, and any sixth former caught with layers of net or tulle under her uniform summer dress was likely to be told to strip. She threatened to hang a row of the offending petticoats like trophies on the hooks outside her office. One of Miss Forster's favourite texts, regularly read out to the whole school in morning assembly, was St Paul's epistle to the Corinthians. As a first former, the bit about charity 'not being puffed up' made me picture the sixth formers sadly deflated by the removal of their petticoats.

Nonetheless, I admired and respected Miss Forster. When I won prizes, I loved being invited into her study which had beautiful old furniture and was tastefully furnished in lavender greys. It reminded me a bit of Maria's bedroom in *The Little White Horse*. Even then, I was impressed by Miss Forster's passion for history and heritage. She cherished the illustrious past of Malvern Hall, and its connections with Constable, who had painted both the house and a portrait of Henry Greswold Lewis, owner of the property in the 1780s. It was Flora Forster who appreciated the Coade stone statues which had graced the property in the past. She restored two of them to niches in the entrance gates and understood the value of another two imposing figures which had stood on pedestals on each side of the entrance. As a young pupil I found these highly romantic, alongside two marble statues of young girls in the entrance hall. One of the latter, slightly kitsch, had flowery garlands. The other showed a girl weeping for the loss of a pet bird which had expired and lay dead in her lap at the end of a silken thread. I now suppose this was Lesbia, lamenting the death of her pet sparrow. Some would read this as a lament for lost virginity. We learned about Catullus in Greek lessons, albeit in a highly expurgated form, but I didn't make the connection until much later.

Much of this is with the benefit of hindsight: in spite of my then grudging respect for Miss Forster, I was aware of a need to contest the values of genteel femininity which the school encouraged. To many of us, regulations about the wearing of gloves and hats and never eating ice-cream in the streets seemed silly. And then there was domestic science, with its attendant humiliations. We had to do needlework and cookery. In needlework we were made to sew 'cookery aprons' in coarse cardboardy cotton with an ugly gingham trim. Horrible matching caps made us look like nippies (waitresses) in a Lyons' Corner House. Domestic science had an uneasy status in a selective, academic high school. We noticed that the domestic science mistresses, unlike the rest of our teachers, never wore gowns in assembly. Many years later, researching the history of girls' education, I learned that in the 1900s, the Girls' Public Day School Trust, pressured by the Board of Education to introduce domestic training into the curriculum in the schools they administered, had refused. But state schools had often no choice in the matter and had generally – albeit reluctantly – complied.

Many of us loathed domestic science and considered it a waste of time. Some years later I read *The Female Eunuch*. Acknowledging the weirdness of girls' schools basing their curriculum on that of boys but then cramming in 'fatuous' subjects like domestic science, Germaine Greer sympathised with the schoolgirl who she pictured 'in her absurd version of masculine uniform, making sponge fingers with inky hands'. She 'must really feel like the punching bag of civilisation', Greer continued. I enjoyed a pleasing shock of recognition.

There were further humiliations around domestic science and needlework. I had passed my eleven-plus a year early and was the youngest in my form. I still had a prepubescent body. We were made to pair up for dressmaking, in order to measure each other's vital statistics. This was fine for those with average measurements but mortifying for the fat girls and for those who were weedy like me. The average bust measurement in the class was something like 34 or 36 inches: my partner measured mine at 25. She giggled, the class giggled, even the needlework teacher looked amused.

Being female had started to feel seriously problematic, both at school and back home. At home, my brothers weren't expected to do anything in the way of domestic chores. I resented them, and especially my mother, for differentiating between us and for being soft on the boys. Ponies and horse-riding provided an escape in these years. The stable yard was a refuge from girliness, and equestrian dress offered a delightful kind of drag: jodhpurs with tight boots and a well-tailored hacking jacket felt liberating, and I liked the idea of a hairnet, a well-brushed bowler and a buttonhole.

School trundled on with low-level but incessant guerrilla warfare over dress and ladylike behaviour as we grew older. We could choose books for school prizes. I realised that I was pushing the boat out a bit when instead of one of the classics, I asked for a book on show jumping by Daphne Machin Goodall. I got away with it. I still have the book, embossed in gold with the school crest. Miss Forster, who knew a lot about adolescent girls, wouldn't have batted an eyelid. But by then she had retired and her successor conspicuously failed to measure up to her in wisdom, taste and personality. I remember her wearing shocking pink Courtelle suits in assembly. Avowing 'modernity', this new headmistress had briskly repudiated elements of the school's heritage, and worst of all in my eyes, she got rid of the statues. I could never forgive her for that.

All sorts of resentments festered. We began to look at boys with more interest than previously, even the noisy and silly ones we encountered on the bus home. This brought even more self-consciousness about looks. Girls queued in the toilets after the bell went at 4pm. They backcombed their hair in order to perch the hated hats precariously, as far back on the head as possible, and applied tinted Clearasil to camouflage adolescent spots. There were daily fights with teachers over details of school uniform.

At weekends I would go with a friend to a local coffee bar. Well, I say 'a' local coffee bar but there was no choice, it was the only one. It was no more than a tiny greasy spoon café in a village about a mile and a half away, a rather sad haunt, but it did have a juke box. I could dress up in my hairy purple mohair skirt, tight polo neck sweater and pointy shoes. My friend and I experimented with talking to one or two of the local boys, but the conversation was terribly stilted and never went anywhere. Once I came home on the back of a boy's motorbike and my father was appalled. There was an occasional 'disco' in the local church hall. This was a sorry affair, too. We were all paralysed with self-consciousness. Dad insisted on picking me up at 9.30pm and was critical if I wore too much eye make-up.

Looking back, I can see clearly that my slow-budding sexuality coincided with some kind of crisis in my parents' marriage. Dad had a certain image of femininity which was at odds with how my mother saw things. Four children and incessant housework tired her out. Dad, inspired by his role as provider, wanted to give her luxuries: jewellery, a fur coat, elegant clothes. Mum, knackered, oozed hostility. They probably didn't talk much about this but I'm pretty sure the conflict put paid to their sex life. I remember Dad coming home with what he thought was a desirable gift: a pale yellow, frothy, lace-trimmed negligée. Mum was horrified. I felt sorry for Dad but could instinctively understand both points of view. I admired Dad's gift and said I found it pretty: Mum threw it across the room and told me I could have it; she had no time for such nonsense. Consigned to the dressing-up box, the thing soon disappeared.

My father was generous though, in that, encouraged by my mother, he decided to give me a regular clothing allowance. Mum had long agonised about me turning out 'too bookish and always thinking too much' and desperately wanted to see more evidence of what she thought of as 'more normal' for a teenage girl: that is, an interest in clothes and boyfriends. As far as I can remember I was given £5 a month: equivalent to about £108 a month today. It enabled me to take a train into Birmingham in order to walk around Richard Shops and C&A. I recently re-read Emma Tennant's memoir of growing up in the 1950s and 1960s, *Girlitude*. Tennant, from a wealthy and privileged background, dressed either in '*couture*', or in clothes 'run up' by the family dressmaker. This was a time when 'the poor', she recalled, 'struggle along dismal pavements with little but C&A or Richard Shops to sustain them'. Well, I certainly didn't feel poor on my new allowance. Synthetic fabrics in bright, citrusy colours were all the rage at the time. I bought a lemon-coloured, spongey-feeling Courtelle coat and wore it with long boots. And a blue woollen sheath dress with a rose at the neck in matching satin, in a little wreath of real mink fur. These little rose brooches surrounded by fur were fashionable in the early 1960s and 'vintage' examples can still be found. Looking at them today, it is hard not to see them as suggestive of female private parts.

My adolescent body continued to generate anxiety. Sweaty armpits that left dark stains; armpit and pubic hair. Deodorants like Odorono didn't work very well and many women still sewed little pads into the arms of dresses ('dress-shields') to soak up sweat and protect clothing. We had dinky little Ladyshave razors in tiny plastic boxes a couple of inches long. They came in pale pink, baby blue or primrose yellow. One summer I spent some of my clothing allowance on a beautiful new swimsuit from C&A: ice-blue, and the synthetic material had a slightly sparkly, iridescent quality. I'd tried it on and thought it looked good, but stepping into the sea I was mortified to discover that the fabric went see-through when wet. As I crept up the beach, everyone could see the dark triangle of my pubic hair. I had to hasten back to the hotel where I hacked the hair off with nail scissors and set to work with the minuscule Ladyshave, suffering an itchy rash for days afterwards.

Shopping trips to C&A didn't completely replace home dressmaking. Most of my friends were reasonably competent at making their own clothes. Many of us haunted the paper pattern sections of the village haberdashery or nearest department store where the latest offerings from Simplicity, Butterick or Vogue were featured in loose-leaf books with plastic coverings, chained to the counter like medieval Bibles. I thought a lot about what I could run up on my mother's sewing machine: most of my ideas were romantic. I remember a white satin 'dolly' dress, with an empire line. The bodice was covered in tiny frills of overlapping lace. I think I only wore it once. It was hugely impractical. I recently read an early novel by Margaret Drabble, *The Garrick Year* (1964). The heroine wears a black velvet suit with a blouse that she has made herself, the front and cuffs of which were 'covered in tiny, thick-starched lace frills'. It had taken her weeks to make and she was very proud of its 'archaic, Victorian photograph quality'. I think I must have been aiming at something similar but would not, at that time, have had the sophistication or the means to go for a black velvet suit.

Simple things worked best. I made a loose, tent-shaped dress with long sleeves out of gorgeous silky stuff printed in bold, swirling psychedelic colours. As a university student in the late 1960s, many of us continued to make clothes. Our all-female hall of residence provided sewing machines. And there were many 'formal' balls and celebratory occasions, for which we

CHAPTER ONE

Home-made dress in silky Tricel fabric, with swirly colours.
With my brother Chris, 1960s.

constructed long, ambitious ballgowns out of cheap materials like lining silk. I ran one up in red lining taffeta; it had an empire line and puffed sleeves. The seams were a bit of a mess on the inside. It was common to start making something like this a day or two before the event. I remember making a raincoat, too, out of a sort of vinyl material covered in tiny forget-me-nots which I wore with white plastic boots, I think from Freeman Hardy & Willis, the nearest I ever got to Courrèges in the sixties. My imagination often ran away with me, I think. Rather a lot of the clothes I made ended up botched and bundled at the back of the wardrobe.

My years as an undergraduate coincided with the revving up of the 'Teenage Revolution'. I remember that when I went for university entrance interviews, my mother was insistent that I should wear what she called 'a costume' or a tailored two-piece. I fell in with this, managing to get something suitable from Richard Shops. It was wool, in dark, forest green with a kind of battledress top. The skirt was just on the knee. But once I left home all hell was let loose, sartorially, as I experimented enthusiastically and chaotically with various styles. I instantly abandoned the kind of demure, efficient typist get-up that Mum thought suitable, and went for miniskirts and boots (almost always referred to as 'kinky' boots at the time). I remember that at home I had expressed a distinct sympathy with Christine Keeler and particularly the witty Mandy Rice-Davies in the early 1960s. Mandy Rice-Davies had lived very close to us: she sounded smart and funny in the papers. My views on such subjects had driven my father spare. Poor Dad. He softened quite a lot as the years passed, though my values and opinions, not to mention style of dress, must have constituted a terrible challenge. Mum confessed some years later that on one occasion they had driven down to Reading (where I was a student) to take me out for lunch. I had greeted them wearing my mum's wedding dress (cut down, the ivory slipper silk train brutally hacked off at the back of the knee... how could I have done this?), accessorised with a fox-fur stole, tails clipped into the fox's head's mouth, along with a blood red rose... Dad had buried his head in his hands, Mum recalled, and slumped over his steering wheel. But he rallied.

Wearing a Lee Bender Bus Stop sweater, Cambridge, 1970s

These were years of radical change in dress codes, particularly amongst the young. In the history department at Reading after the war, Lady Doris Stenton, wife of the Anglo-Saxon historian Sir Frank Stenton, had set the tone: she had strongly disapproved of women undergraduates wearing trousers. Undergraduates were expected to wear gowns in hall for formal dinner. The disapproval of trousers for women didn't survive the 1960s, although on formal dining occasions they could still cause eyebrows to lift and some restaurants banned them. One or two bold spirits, challenged at the door for wearing trouser suits, offered to remove the trousers and to dine wearing just the jacket as a micro skirt. This usually had the desired effect, unnerving any officious doormen.

I did a year of teacher training before going on to postgraduate study. Some schools were tough on what we could wear in the classroom. Short hair for young men, no trousers for young women. In one school I was taken to task for wearing too much eye make-up (I had developed what was to be a lifetime's habit of ringing my eyes with kohl). There was more trouble over skirt length, at a time when fashion was swinging pendulum-like in a deranged way between mini and maxi skirts. It was a relief to get back to university, where by the early 1970s you could pretty much wear what you liked. But what *did* I like? I remember this as a time when I was often and increasingly unsure. I made what I think was my last effort in the way of home dressmaking at that time, a fully lined blue dress in a filmy pale blue floral material, its neckline and hem bordered in fine, graduated bands of pale blue velvet. It was very pretty and much admired, but I felt daft in it. Milk-maidy. Wrong. So I never wore it, and passed it on to a fellow student. From then on, I bought clothes in bolder designs from shops like Etam, Biba and Bus Stop. There was a dress by Ossie Clark which I loved, in red-and-black crepe, cut on the bias. I think it was by Ossie Clark for Radley; I wish I'd kept it. Biba had huge appeal, those clingy dresses in fabrics the colour of wine-gums or bottled fruit. I confess to having worn hot pants: in black, with tiny flowers and a drawstring waist. A bit like a baby's romper suit, but oddly, wearing them felt liberating. You could stride out in them with bare legs and not worry about stockings or tights.

With hindsight I can see that being unsure about my taste in clothes at this time was bound up with insecurity about what I was going to do with my life, whether to embark upon a PhD or to try to get some sort of teaching job. I couldn't really imagine other options. There wasn't much career advice in higher education in the early 1970s. Before the Sex Discrimination Act of 1975, university appointments services were divided into men's and women's sections and the limited opportunities offered to women undergraduates were legendary. I remember vividly my interview with a careers advisory officer at Reading. She suggested teaching or a traineeship with something called The Metal Box Company. I was offered a paid fellowship to study for a doctorate following my MA at Lancaster but there was talk about a shortage of academic teaching jobs, so when I was offered a lectureship in history at what was then Bristol Polytechnic, it seemed sensible to go for it.

I had visited Bristol for the job interview and was overwhelmed by the gorgeousness of Clifton. Living in a rented flat in Princess Victoria Street seemed like heaven. I settled down to the teaching, which required a lot of preparation, and forged close friendships with two women, Helen Taylor and Madge Dresser, which have lasted to this day. We were a small group of three, then, in a largely all-male environment. I have a blurry photo of us, from that time, standing outside the house (then owned by the architect, Berthold Lubetkin) in Princess Victoria Street. Madge and I are clad in jeans, Helen wears an Afghan embroidered dress, striped in dark blue and magenta pink. I wore what became a kind of uniform of black velvet jacket and rose- or wine-coloured needlecord jeans just about every day through my time in Bristol. The main concession to femininity was an artificial rose or bunch of violets in the buttonhole. It felt comfortable and somehow right. Jeans were good because you could wear flat shoes or comfortable low-heeled boots. You could drive in these or walk for miles. No faffing around with heels and sore feet.

After a short time in Bristol I moved to Brighton, hoping that a lectureship at the University of Sussex would give me more space for research. I wore a skirt and demure blouse for the interview, I remember, but soon reverted to jacket and jeans. Brighton was awash with fashionable boutiques and I soon branched out into 1940s-style little V-necked sweaters

A favourite Bus Stop sweater, 1970s

in bright colours, with Fair Isle patterns and slightly puffed sleeves. I had sweaters in black and silver chevron stripes, and a slightly tarty one in red edged in black, which I particularly loved, with a little loop at the neck. I still have it, though the wool is now lumpy and matted: I can't bear to throw it away.

I met Nick von Tunzelmann, whom I was to marry, at an academic conference. He was an economic historian, and a lecturer in Cambridge. He approved of my academic ambitions, which was most unusual in my experience of men up to that time. Academic Cambridge was very different from Brighton. On formal occasions men and women might even dine separately: men in formal academic dress, drinking like fish and on occasions throwing pudding at each other. (It was rumoured that in one college there was a special recipe for something called 'Wibbly Pudding', designed for drunken lobbing.) Women might eat presided over by the Master's wife, no academic dress, very polite. Or there might be gender segregation after mixed dining and dessert. The atmosphere was very public school and middle class and, of course, male. There were all sorts of odd customs designed to put outsiders and the uninitiated into a defensive position: which way to pass the port, what to do with snuff, bowls of rosewater and snowy napkins after dinner, not lighting a cigarette until the youngest Fellow in the room had done so, etc. (I may have made this last custom up but similar rules existed, everywhere.)

The talk of admitting women into male colleges amplified the misogyny of some male academics in both Oxford and Cambridge in the 1970s. This wasn't new. In the 1960s, Dacre Balsdon, a fellow of Exeter, had imagined a future in which the fellows of an all-male college, forced to admit women, barricaded themselves in the wine cellars, drinking through their entire contents before setting the college on fire rather than see it 'desecrated' by a female presence. Ten years later the movement for co-education had gained traction and feelings were sharply divided. Many of those in the women's colleges were as hostile to the idea of mixed colleges as the men: they feared losing their own strongholds, they feared that women might lose out. I was to research and write about all this many years later. It wasn't easy being female in Cambridge in the 1970s, as many female academics have attested.

What did academic women wear? In the long struggle to gain access to the ancient universities, they had regularly been advised to dress cautiously and modestly, so as to look unthreatening. A disdain for feminine adornment could sometimes get out of hand. Many female students despaired at the fusty, down-at-heel appearance of their high-minded women tutors. Alice Gardner, a history tutor at Newnham, became legendary for looking unkempt. There's a story from the early years of the last century that on one occasion, travelling by train, she sat down on a bench, took off her hat and nodded off. When she awoke, she found her hat full of small change. There were some exceptions. Younger women dons might dress with flair; others developed a strong personal style. Scholar of French literature Enid Starkie roamed round the pubs in Oxford in the 1950s and 60s wearing red slacks and a beret, smoking a cigar. There goes Enid, 'in all the colours of the Rimbaud', quipped classical scholar and Warden of Wadham, Maurice Bowra. In the 1900s, students who expressed strong individuality through dress were often gently (or not so gently) discouraged. Dorothy Sayers is said to have once appeared at breakfast in Somerville with a red ribbon in her hair and a pair of earrings featuring scarlet and green parrots in tiny gilt cages. The Principal deputed a fellow student to get her to take them off.

As a regular visitor and sometime resident of Cambridge in the 1970s, it seemed to me that scholarly women there had developed a recognisable style: sensible, unobtrusive, middle class. Skirt length just below the knee, to facilitate bicycle riding. Comfortable, flat sandals. Shirtwaisters. Print fabrics. Very little make-up. I felt somewhat conspicuous in my blacks and reds, boots and miniskirts, eyes rimmed in kohl. I was aware that the style might look a bit 'vulgar' in the eyes of some, but somehow it was becoming part of my identity, and I stuck to it. A more serious challenge came from some of the feminist groups I was associated with at that time. I remember, for instance, going to a talk at A Woman's Place, then housed in Hungerford House on the Victoria Embankment. As usual, I was wearing perfume and a fair amount of eye make-up. At some point I became aware that I was the only person there wearing any make-up and that almost everyone apart from me was dressed in Mao-style jackets and dark blue denim. I went to the loo, spat on a tissue and tried to remove some of the mascara and eye black. Then I recalled that I had done this twice before. Once, when as a teacher trainee I had been told to do so by a bossy older teacher, and before that, at a church hall hop in my early teens just before my disapproving father was due to collect me at 9.30pm. Oh heck, I thought to myself, you should have the guts not to internalise proscriptions and to dress as you like.

Pregnancy was a big challenge, in a number of ways. It came at a time when many of my husband's colleagues (and probably both of our families) expected that I would move to Cambridge and assume a wifely role of support. But I was just beginning to establish myself at Sussex and the thought of this independence slipping away from me was scary. We decided to continue living in two places, and to share childcare. It was quite a radical decision at the time. My husband was quizzed about it in college. 'Is it really necessary, in this day and age, to have two incomes?' he was asked by the then Master. The Master's wife visited me in the small house we had rented from the College. She was very kind, but it was as if she was the Lady of the Manor and I was a humble cottager.

I remember feeling terribly uncertain about how to dress and behave in pregnancy. Flowery smocks from chain-store Mothercare were out. I hadn't taken to those frilly, floral milk-maid outfits from Laura Ashley that had been so popular a few years earlier. There was no way I could have worn such things. I searched everywhere for skirts with expandable waistbands in black. I didn't find it easy to repress a surge of hostility to the well-meaning health workers who addressed me as 'Mum' and talked reverently about 'Baby'. I baulked at being defined by motherhood.

I am thankful that I never experienced anything in the nature of postnatal depression: rather, a surge of unanticipated delight in my baby girls. I think this may have been because I had worried so much in advance about the problems of being a mother, and its impact on my identity, and had overlooked the pleasures. Much to my surprise, I thoroughly enjoyed having young children. Our daughters were intelligent and funny, a stimulus to creativity, an excuse to play, a perpetual source of wonder and joy. Nick was a besotted and completely engaged father; he never reneged on his promise of sharing childcare. The only problem was exhaustion, for both of us, which was serious, but didn't last for ever. The exhaustion did mean that I thought less about clothes, though. I tended, for a while, to dress as if for combat. I had a couple of stylish boiler suits, one in dark grey needlecord, another in grey blue, which I wore tightly belted. And I particularly remember a fur-lined pair of 'tractor boots'. They were from ECCO, and extremely comfortable. I wore them with leggings and a black sweater, most of the time.

As the girls grew up, they started to experiment with their own style and identities. As children, they alternated between a girly femininity and a more practical can't-be-bothered approach. They were capable of swooning over princess-y stuff – Errol Le Cain's wonderful illustrations for fairy stories like *The Twelve Dancing Princesses*, or sugary Barbie doll outfits, but keen also to dress as dinosaurs, Superwoman or goths. Wednesday Addams was an inspiration for my younger daughter, Eugénie, who was also fond of dressing as Xena: Warrior Princess. Both girls loved dressing up, and Halloween parties, allowing space for a camp ghoulishness, were a riot. By early adolescence it was clear that both daughters had developed a quite sophisticated understanding of the meanings of clothes: they both would tease me about my own style and its relation to feminism. We were a household of *Guardian* readers and had long enjoyed cartoons by Posy Simmonds: we bought all the books which collected her cartoons together in the 1980s. A favourite was Mrs Weber's Diary, featuring down-at-heel polytechnic lecturer George Weber and his family. George's wife, Wendy, wore round spectacles a bit like mine and long skirts and sweaters (not like me at all). She cobbled together her own style of motherhood. Their daughter, Belinda, went in for sharper hairstyles and edgier and sexier clothes as she reached her teenage years and I'm pretty sure our eldest daughter identified with her. My daughters started to exert some influence over the way I dressed from the 1980s on. They were disconcertingly observant and teased me for occasionally going in for unsuitable sweaters in red or bobbly knitted orange, suggesting that I was particularly likely to make bad decisions when premenstrual. Alex could draw very well, and produced some wickedly unsparing cartoons of her parents, her sister and herself.

One might think that by the 1980s and 90s I would have become more confident in my dress sense, but far from it. I think that my attitude to clothes became seriously deranged in these decades. I bought lots and lots of clothes and wore some of them very few times. Two things were unsettling me. First, I began to think about promotion at work, which I knew would be a terrible struggle – it still wasn't easy for women in universities, even if they earned a reputation for teaching (not necessarily seen as an advantage back then), even if they published quite a lot, even if they got grants. It was clearly going to be a long uphill battle and one I wasn't sure of winning. Second, as some of my energy returned after the years of parental exhaustion, I rediscovered my sexuality. So, too, did my husband. Sadly, because I don't think we ever stopped loving and supporting each other, this was a time of great difficulty between us. We worked out some kind of compromise, eventually, but I still look back on many aspects of this experience with pain and regret.

I oscillated between trying to look like a career woman and what I hoped was a kind of ageing sexiness. The two were often in conflict. Surveys showed that universities were particularly bad at promoting women in the 1980s, but things were difficult in other professions, too. I had friends who worked as GPs or in hospital medicine. I recall a conversation with one of the latter who aimed at becoming a consultant. We joked about a necessary step being one of abandoning her comfortable dresses for some kind of pinstripe skirt and jacket suit which might look authoritative or 'consultoid'. These were years of women moving towards 'power dressing'. Former editor of British *Vogue*, Alexandra Shulman, points to the assumption, common in the 1980s, that 'clothing for women which mimicked the garb of men would help them climb up the professional ladder'. But in reality, 'fashion was ahead of the game' and promotions still came agonisingly slowly for most women. I remember buying a couple of suits (from M&S), one of which was in a beige linen mixture, the other in black-and-white dog's tooth check with pronounced shoulder pads. But I don't remember getting much wear out of either of them. I think on one occasion I accompanied my girls to a pop concert in the Brighton Centre wearing the dog's tooth outfit. I was surrounded by teenage girls all ecstatic over Matt and Luke Goss, and looked and felt out of place.

As for the sexiness… for the first time in my life I began to spend more money on underwear. This was partly mood, partly wish-fulfilment, I think. Desire and daydreams were surely part of it. Janet Reger's designs for underwear had a huge effect on what became available in the shops from the mid-1980s on, and then came Madonna and the fashion for underwear worn as outerwear. The demand for bustiers and corsets co-existed with that for shoulder pads and power dressing, quite a lot of it aspirational, and probably both compensatory and contradictory at the same time. But that was the late eighties and nineties for you, and my life seemed very much an example of a general trend. Pretty crazy, it was, looking back. And yet it wasn't the first time that fashionable trends seemed almost to undercut social movements. I think back to the suffrage struggles of the 1900s. Those massive plumed hats teetering atop ornate, upswept hairdos, and narrow, constricting 'hobble skirts' just as bicycles were opening up freedoms for women and more and more of them were fighting for the right to vote.

I bought some daft, expensive things at the turn of the millennium. I think I knew, deep down, that these expensive purchases were compelled by illusion, the mistaken hope that they would somehow transform my life. Writer Linda Grant discusses this kind of illusion and the compulsion that goes with it in her insightful book, *The Thoughtful Dresser* (2009), which starts out by trying to make sense of how she felt compelled by an overwhelming 'need', one morning, to go out and buy a pair of expensive and impractical shoes. For me, money was less tight once the children were through education. Amid all the experimentation, I think, I started to consolidate a more personal style. Mainly black. Close fitting. Usually from agnès B. With glitter, or flashes and slashes of red. Bright flashes of colour are needed to lift the draining effects of black as one ages. Red lipstick lifts the spirits and has something of defiance in it. Remember Marlene Dietrich in the film *Dishonoured* (1931): she checks her reflection in the blade of a military sword and re-applies her lipstick before facing the firing squad.

I recently re-read Victoria Glendinning's biography of Rebecca West and was reminded that even someone as intelligent and strong-minded as she was had been familiar with the kind of compulsion which has one 'needing' new items of clothing. For a long time, as a young woman, West was worn down by her relationship with H.G. Wells, her passionate lover and the father of their young son, Anthony. Wells was a man who ruthlessly compartmentalised his life. He had numerous affairs, but remained staunchly married to his second wife Jane, with whom he continued to share a domestic life. Rebecca and her son were hidden away in seaside lodgings, the little boy vaguely thinking his mother his aunt. Awful for Rebecca: indeed, awful for both of them. She confessed that it was a time when she went in for a lot of what we might now call impulse buying, purchasing extravagant 'silk evening knickers', and other such luxuries. Eventually she and Wells parted, but Rebecca's love life thereafter never quite lived up to her dreams. In her mid-eighties, feeling low, we learn that she sought comfort in going shopping with her friend Madge Garland (formerly the Royal College of Art's first professor of fashion). She wanted to cheer herself up with the purchase of a new fur coat.

Highly successful designer and businesswoman Miuccia Prada once shrewdly suggested that much fashion was about 'the desperation of being sexy'. I recognise this in my own life and in the evidence archived in my wardrobe. So many black dresses, red roses and silk poppies. The fur (synthetic, mostly, but I have bits and pieces of real fur from the past), the satin slips and delicate lace and camisoles. An impractical but rather wonderful Vivienne Westwood fine, black mesh body stocking with cavorting shepherds and Rococo swirls over the nipples. Getting older doesn't do away with the sensuousness of this stuff, or with these feelings, however much part of you stands aside, ruefully, thinking of fading flowers and mutton dressed as lamb.

Some years ago, my husband, desperately depleted by Parkinson's disease, had to go into a care home. I learned a lot from regular visits to this place. There was one old lady unsure of who she was any more, but my goodness, she had some beautiful clothes. I remember particularly a soft lavender-coloured cashmere, and a jacket made of devoré silk-velvet, patterned like leopardskin. The wonderful staff dressed her in these lovely things, though they wouldn't have lasted long, given the washing facilities in a care home. It made me wonder what the woman had been like, before she descended into age and infirmity, and whether her clothes helped to remind her of who she was.

CHAPTER ONE

Vivienne Westwood body in black mesh with Rococo swirls

Ah, but identity is complex and shifting, and there's no escaping that. Victoria Glendinning, in a comment on Rebecca West's unfinished novel *Sunflower*, emphasises how much thinly disguised personal experience went into the writing of it. It was drafted when Rebecca was struggling with what was to be the last phase of her ten-year sexual relationship with H.G. Wells, and at a time when she became increasingly focused on her romantic obsession with Lord Beaverbrook. The text mirrors the highly contradictory facets of the author's subjectivity. West was a public intellectual; her brain and wit were legendary. She impressed the majority of her contemporaries as a confident, powerful woman. But we know that this confidence went alongside a profound unease about her sexuality, a fear that she might unman men, reducing them to physical impotence. West was 'a flux of alternative selves', concludes Glendinning, more insecure in her subjectivity than the world ever knew.

I am not good at clearing out my wardrobe; indeed, my several wardrobes. I joke about this. Historians are a bit retentive, I suggest, in Freudian terms, not good at letting go. They harbour, collect and archive stuff, maybe in part because of emotional needs bound up with their investment in the past, part in order to footnote, to make sense of things. But when I peer into the recesses of my many cupboards and storage spaces I quail. It has gone too far, I fear, all this accretion. Is it a bit like an eating disorder or a drink problem? Elizabeth Robins, feminist, writer and celebrated actress in (among other things) Ibsen's plays about women, used to live just round the corner from me in Brighton with her friend, pioneering medical woman Octavia Wilberforce. Angela John, her biographer, tells us that Elizabeth had always been a hoarder. She left 102 packing cases of belongings when she died, and her executors found twenty-five black hats, all in perfect condition. This seems quite modest to me. I am not going to add up the sum of the black dresses I have bought and been unable to throw out: I think the number would shame me.

I'm not as bad as Emily Tinne, the well-off Liverpool matron and wife of a local doctor who has often been labelled Britain's first 'shopaholic'. This lady went shopping every day in the

1930s and bought piles of garments she never even got round to taking out of their tissue-lined boxes. Why, we will never know. Her daughter (who donated a large part of her mother's collection to Liverpool museums), suggested that there was an element of charitableness in the purchases: Mrs Tinne wanted to help the underpaid shop assistants who needed customers to stay in work. Writer Linda Grant suggests that Emily simply got a buzz from shopping. I wonder whether buying outfits helped to sustain a fantasy of a life happier and more fulfilling than her own. Her clothes were her dreams. There can be a strong belief in the transformational power of clothes, their unique ability to make life better for us. Clothes are close to the self. We may imagine ourselves looking different, looking good, confident in a happier and more fulfilling state of affairs.

So, fantasy, hope and desire can all be embodied in how we dress.

Knowing this, and even at my advanced age, I obsess about the possibilities signified by a new pair of boots; a red dress. It is autumn as I write, and a lifetime of working in academia leads me to associate the new term with new beginnings: new pencil cases, new notebooks, new projects. Just when will I learn the limits of these unruly desires? Will I ever? Probably not. Right now I'm off to buy the red dress.

TWO

Crinoline Ladies

I HAVE FLASHES OF MEMORY from my first day at school, when I was four years old. I remember being given a slate and put to drawing. I drew a lady in a crinoline dress, with panniers, and with a flower in her hair. The dress had a scalloped hemline. Adrian, sitting next to me, had short trousers and knobbly knees and he drew a signpost. I couldn't think why.

It wasn't the first time I had drawn a lady in a full skirt, I had done so often at home, and my mum and grandmother had always admired my artwork so I guess I wanted to impress the teacher at my new school. A bit later I produced my first attempt at a book: crudely folded paper with hectic lettering, words spelled entirely phonetically. The story focused on Cinderella and her 'ugle sisdz' [sic], and it was illustrated with – yes – a cover image of Cinderella in a crinoline ballgown, crudely rendered in wax crayons. My mother admired this early attempt at authorship and saved it for posterity. I have the booklet, still.

Crinolines were fashionable in mid-Victorian times; their heyday was in the 1860s. By the 1870s, the shape had gone out of fashion for womenswear, being replaced by looped-back skirts and the bustle. But the shape itself seems to have lingered long in the popular imagination. Particularly in the 1930s, we find it inspiring decoration on china tea sets, chocolate boxes, biscuit tins and embroideries. Printed embroidery designs, especially, regularly featured ladies wearing crinolines and bonnets, sometimes feeding bluebirds, often posed in gardens framed by weeping willows and hollyhocks. These designs were massively popular: antimacassars, napkins and table linen, washbags and the like, embroidered with crinoline lady motifs, are plentifully available today on ebay or in second-hand and antique shops.

Crinoline lady design on box of linen handkerchiefs from the 1950s

The fashion for crinoline ladies and their ubiquity as a design motif continued after the war. If anything, it became even more of a trend, with the success and impact of Dior's New Look after 1947. Dior had extolled the delights of '*le ligne corolle*', designed to make women look like flowers, '*femmes fleurs*', with rounded shoulders, full busts and tiny waists above full, spreading skirts. In spite of the publicity attached to the New Look as a landmark in fashion history, he wasn't the only designer to feature wasp waists and full skirts. A new enthusiasm for such was detected in the United States before the war, and in Britain, in the late 1930s, Queen Elizabeth (later the Queen Mother) had favoured romantic, frothy, bell-shaped gowns designed by Norman Hartnell. These were apparently inspired by Winterhalter's portraits of a crinoline-clad Queen Victoria in the Royal Collection.

What *was* new was the gradual ending of austerity and clothes rationing, which made New Look-type dresses and skirts possible. They took many yards of material. The boxy, square-shouldered and slim-skirted look of the 1940s had required much less. Some tut-tutted at the expense and the wastefulness, not to mention the body-constricting effects of corseted waists and heavy swooshing skirts. But the new silhouette was soon everywhere. The doors of gendered cloakrooms and public lavatories often

Crinoline lady decorating sanitary disposal bag

sported a sort of Madame de Pompadour silhouette signifying 'Ladies'. Even the paper bags designed for sanitary waste in ladies' loos had a design of a crinoline lady on them.

Cinema both fuelled and reflected current fashion trends, as it had done since the 1930s. Film versions of two blockbuster novels were particularly influential: that of Margaret Mitchell's 1936 *Gone with the Wind*, filmed three years later, and Kathleen Winsor's *Forever Amber* (1944) filmed in 1947. These lush costume dramas provided much-needed escapism, particularly to British women who had been forced into skimping and saving on clothes during extended wartime austerity. Scarlett O'Hara's (Vivien Leigh's) dresses in *Gone with the Wind,* designed by Walter Plunkett, epitomised the styles of Southern belles in the 1860s, when the fashion for crinolines with hoop skirts, corsets and pantalettes was at its height. The green-sprigged muslin crinoline with ruffled shoulders and dark green velvet sash, which Scarlett puts on after having been tightly laced into her corset by Mammie, is just one of the gowns in the film which have become legendary. *Forever Amber* is set in the seventeenth rather than the nineteenth century; its luscious, off-the-shoulder and full-skirted dresses are breathtaking. The clothes in the film have been described by feminist writer Elaine Showalter as 'marvels of fashion pornography'. At one event Amber is resplendent in cloth-of-gold and emerald velvet, her cloak is lined in sable and she wears 'a spray of emeralds pinned to her sable muff'. This was heady stuff for women who had sparingly improvised dresses out of curtain material, parachute silk or old blankets.

The British film studio Gainsborough Pictures was responsible for a series of hugely popular costume melodramas in the early 1940s. Founded in 1924 by Michael Balcon, the Gainsborough studios were based first in Islington, then Hoxton. Their films featured an opening cameo of a fine lady (Celia Bird, later Glennis Lorimer) in an oval frame, the lady resplendent in eighteenth-century period costume, her elaborate plumed hat perched above a riot of towering and tumbling curls. The cameo was supposedly based on Thomas Gainsborough's portrait of Sarah Siddons. This opening logo has the lady bow her head, graciously and somehow conspiratorially, towards the audience: it is almost a shared acknowledgment that what follows will be fantasy, and fantasy of the most extravagant, worldly kind. Gainsborough costume dramas – e.g. *The Man in Grey* (1943), *Fanny by Gaslight* (1944), *The Wicked Lady* and *Madonna of the Seven Moons* (both 1945) – featured wilful heroines driven by lust and greed: they offered potent escapist fantasies to wartime women. The luxurious period costumes designed by Elizabeth Haffenden – low-cut, richly embellished bodices, nipped-in waists and billowing silk and satin skirts – were a key part of the appeal. The Gainsborough melodramas had fallen out of fashion by the end of the war, but the costume details impacted on the popular imagination, preparing the ground for the rapturous reception of Dior's New Look at the end of the decade.

The New Look didn't please everybody. There were feminists who were uneasy about it as romanticising a past when women were constrained by ample, heavy skirts and tight corseting. A huge amount of material was needed to construct New Look dresses – as much as 25 yards (23m) in some examples. In Britain, the President of the Board of Trade, Sir Stafford Cripps, is said to have inveighed against the sheer profligacy of it. But the graceful lines and opulent femininity of the new silhouette exerted a powerful appeal. Princess Margaret was a devotee: she was photographed in an off-the-shoulder Dior New Look gown for her twenty-first birthday in 1951: seven layers of creamy organza silk over a 22½ inch (55cm) waist, the boned bodice and top layer of the skirt embellished with sequins, raffia, rhinestones and mother-of-pearl. She looked every inch the fairy princess. Cinderella-at-the-ball, fairytale gowns haunted the romantic imagination of many women in the 1950s, images intensified by the wedding of Princess Elizabeth and Philip Mountbatten in 1947 and the Coronation in 1953.

The sumptuousness of postwar *couture* could be staggering. Fashion journalist Alison Settle, writing for the *Observer* in 1952, recognised that such clothes were for the very few. Marvelling at the Balmain collection in August 1952, she averred that 'No store buyer could hope to repeat such richness nor copy the fur coats lined with lace mounted over chiffon and often decorated with pearls.' Even so, the elaborate *couture* gowns and costumes by Dior were objects of desire and fantasy for many women. Historian Carolyn Steedman has confessed that it was with the image of a New Look coat in 1950 that she made her first attempt to understand her mother's desires and longings. In Paul Gallico's popular novel, *Flowers for Mrs Harris* (1958), Ada Harris, a London charlady, falls in love with a Dior dress hanging in the wardrobe of one of her employers. She scrimps and saves until she has enough money to go to Paris and purchase a Dior gown for herself: it is her heart's desire simply to own such a garment. Surmounting all odds, Mrs Harris arrives at the Dior salon in Paris to make her choice. The dress she chooses is called 'Temptation'. The skirt is in floor-length black velvet embellished with jet beads, the bodice 'a froth of cream, delicate pink and white chiffon, tulle and lace'. The dress made the young girl modelling it look like a cross between Venus rising from the sea foam and a woman emerging from tousled bedclothes. Gallico tells us that she was clothed 'most decently and morally' and yet looked 'wholly indecent and overwhelmingly alluring'. Acquiring this dress changes Mrs Harris's life in many unpredictable and heart-warming ways, although she never gets to wear it.

Most women, of course, made do with lesser fantasies, either running up their own Dior-style dresses from paper patterns (Alison Settle tells us that in the early 1950s, American women made on average about twelve dresses a year at home) or they bought store copies. Particularly popular were ready-to-wear dresses by British manufacturer Horrockses, based in Lancashire. Horrockses Fashions produced day and evening dresses, housecoats and beachwear. Their day dresses, with New Look-type full skirts, nipped-in waists and tailored bodices, sold well. They were produced in washable cottons ('cool and crisp'), printed with a wide range of designs: roses, bows and bands of print known as *bayadère*. Kathleen Molyneux, sister of designer Edward Molyneux, worked as a *directrice* of Horrockses in the 1950s, and their house designer John Tullis had trained at Molyneux in Paris. The firm used modern designers, such as Eduardo Paolozzi, Graham Sutherland and Alastair Morton, sometimes experimenting with bold prints inspired by Africa or the Caribbean.

Horrockses Fashions' casual, soft and practical version of the New Look was marketed in the United States as well as in Britain, and their dresses featured in upmarket fashion magazines, including *Vogue*. Settle sang their praises. Following a show of their new lines 'in a white room, trellised with velvety red roses' in 1952, she reported in her column in the *Observer*: 'Here were dresses which, for beauty of line, colour and fabric, were breathtaking.' There were 'afternoon models' and evening dresses as well as the crisp cottons, in silks, satins, 'matelassé rayons' and nylons, dreamy dresses that would retail at 14 to 18 guineas when they reached the shops. This was still too expensive for most women, of course. The cotton dresses (between £4 and £7) were considerably cheaper. Queen Elizabeth packed dresses from Horrockses on her tour of the Commonwealth in 1953–54.

Dior's *'ligne corolle'* and what he called his 'Princess line' of 1951 required figure control. Corsetry might be needed to produce what Settle called 'the poured in look'. 'There is certainly no

CHAPTER TWO

Horrockses sundress, 1950s

Horrockses dress with bayadère design

extraneous aid for the less-than-slim figure in this line,' she wrote, referring to the Princess line in her column for the *Observer* in August 1952. The Princess line might have narrower skirts, but full skirts were far from finished. At a fashion show featuring London *couture* leaders hosted by Lady Clark in Hampstead in November 1953, with both the Queen Mother and Princess Margaret in attendance, designers including Charles Creed, Digby Morton, Hardy Amies and Victor Stiebel were represented. There were many 'vast-skirted dresses' on show, some requiring up to 80 yards (73m) of fabric.

Dior kept changing the line and silhouette of his clothes with each collection before his death in 1957. The Princess line was followed by the 'H line' in the mid-fifties, then the 'A line', the 'Y line', the 'F line'. Hemlines went up and down, with fashion journalists writing in some confusion about 'the battle of the hemlines', and leading to a dizzying series of headlines.

The younger generation, reasonably oblivious to the dictates of *haute couture*, took to the circle skirt. Said to have been 'invented' by Juli Lynne Charlot in the US around the same time as Dior's New Look (1947), the circle skirt was originally cut from felt and decorated with whimsical felt appliqué motifs: small dogs and cats, wine glasses and what-have-you, with poodles perhaps the most popular. Circle (or poodle) skirts needed bulking out with petticoats for the required effect. These petticoats, in tiered nylon net or tulle gave a can-can or crinoline effect, and stiffened, rustled round the legs.

I wrote earlier about how these petticoats were banned in the girls' grammar school I attended for the first time in 1959–60. I was a gawky child at the time, having barely approached adolescence. I never had a proper circle skirt but I did have a bunchy flared one in mohair, dark purple and green. I wore it with a stiffened petticoat and a wide, patent-leather belt. My mother had her 'dinner dresses', all of which had very full, semi-crinoline-type skirts. She didn't wear them very often, just on the few occasions when she and my father went to dinner dances or special evening dos. She certainly had Horrockses-type summer dresses with bands of decorative print, though whether or not these were genuine Horrockses I have no idea.

Silhouettes were changing, though, under the influence of Quant and the Teenage Revolution. I don't remember wearing any more ballerina-type, big skirts again. Only once, maybe, at my wedding. This was a white cotton full-skirted dress from a shop called Mexicana, in Chelsea. It had bell-sleeves and was banded with pin tucks and lace. Early in the present century, there was something of a fifties fashion revival. It coincided to some extent with the popularity of the television series, *Mad Men*. There was a fashion for cupcakes, and for dresses with a distinctly cupcake air about them. The fashion extended to floral designs on china and homeware. But I was having none of it.

THREE

School Uniforms

THE HISTORY OF GIRLS' SCHOOL UNIFORM is a history of controversy, confusion and semiotic chaos. It carries a messy entanglement of meanings, fought out on generations of girls' bodies. Teachers have regularly 'policed' girls' uniforms to what might seem heights (or depths) of ludicrousness. Many of us can remember being made to kneel on the floor in order to have our skirt lengths measured, or having to attest to the thickness of stockings, the colour of underwear, the wearing of hats at a certain angle. With some teachers, a note of irony might creep in: a joking rather than a shaming. My daughters recalled a teacher who stood at the door as the girls filed into assembly droning 'illegal socks', 'illegal scrunchies' (hair ties) in a slightly bored voice, but not doing much more about it.

There were divided – even opposing – motives for the introduction of uniform in girls' schools. It was once promoted as liberating, particularly in the days when young women wore corsets, tight blouses and long skirts. Then, some longed for the kind of clothes that would allow girls to exercise in the gym or to run free on the playing field. School uniform has often been argued to promote social equality, and to distract girls from obsessing over the petty details of fashion and what to wear. It has been further defended as a way of engendering institutional loyalties and corporate spirit. On the other hand, uniform has been seen as socially demeaning, an insult to individuality, an imposition of unwelcome class and gender norms, even as an assault upon personal liberty. These contradictions are rendered even more complicated by the fact that girls' school uniforms have become associated with fancy dress and dressing-up games; with transgression, lesbianism and pornography.

Many of these meanings lurked or were made explicit in the German film *Mädchen in Uniform*, Leontine Sagan's wonderfully expressive film of 1931. The film was made in the context of the Weimar Republic's open questioning of ideas about sexual identity and debate around politics before Hitler's rise to power in 1933. It was subsequently banned, and Goebbels ordered the destruction of all existing copies in Germany. The film explores the atmosphere in a girls' boarding school ruled by an autocratic headmistress. Girls – several of them from Prussian military families – are drilled like soldiers and relentlessly monitored, expected to submit to a battery of inflexible rules. The school functions as a total institution. On entry, girls found themselves stripped of their own clothes and made to wear dresses in a coarse striped material, covered by drab aprons. Hair had to be tightly dressed, never to overhang the collar. The striped dresses bring to mind the uniforms suffragettes were required to wear in British prisons, or even the striped uniforms later forced on prisoners in Nazi concentration camps. The aim was to erase the person, to create a subordinate category of human being. The disgust felt by inmates at having to endure the unpleasantness of rough, scratchy and previously worn clothing was part of the process of ritual submission and humiliation.

Food and comforts are scarce in the school featured in Sagan's film, but girls are prohibited from writing home to complain. When one girl attempts this, her letter is confiscated and she is punished. Homoeroticism flourishes in the emotionally austere environment of this school, with the girls having crushes particularly on the most sympathetic and attractive young teacher, Fräulein von Bernburg. In the dormitory, von Bernburg regularly kisses each girl goodnight, and they swoon over it. The motherless central character, Manuela, falls hopelessly in love with this teacher, and it is her indiscretion in openly boasting of their mutual attraction, after a few too many drinks, that provokes a major crisis. The school's headmistress resorts to a series of harsh and punitive measures designed to isolate Manuela socially and emotionally, and which eventually provoke the girl to attempt suicide. Faced with this, the inmates rebel: they gang up against the inhumanity of it all and the system breaks down. The defeat of the headmistress and her disciplinary system signifies a victory for the values of friendship, compassion and love.

In *Mädchen in Uniform*, uniformity is associated with a lack of social status and repression. In Victorian Britain, many middle-class girls were educated at home, and the question of wearing anything like a uniform simply didn't arise. Girl pupils in charity schools might wear caps and aprons, but this would be considered fitting, since their poverty and social class meant that they were destined for domestic service on leaving. For girls whose sense of dignity or respectability coexisted with straitened circumstances, uniform could be acutely humiliating. We may recall the Brontë sisters' experiences of being sent to the Clergy Daughters' School at Cowan Bridge in the 1820s, an experience later drawn upon by Charlotte in her description of Lowood in *Jane Eyre*. The sisters found the regulation uniform, the serviceable woollen dresses, the straw cottage bonnets and brown holland pinafores, hard to endure.

As a movement for more purposeful – even academic – training for girls gained traction in late nineteenth-century Britain, new schools for girls were established and the question of what pupils should wear came to the fore. Many middle-class parents undoubtedly found the idea of their daughters being required to wear anything like a uniform degrading:

unladylike and unacceptable. They were feepayers, so their views counted. Celebrated headmistress and founder of the North London Collegiate School, Frances Buss, is said to have been sympathetic to the idea of introducing uniform, but did not think that she would be able to get away with it. In the early days of her career she had to content herself by waging war against 'unsuitable ornamentation'; lace or jewellery in the morning being a particular bugbear.

Attitudes to girls' dress did begin to change, however, in response to the growing enthusiasm for physical education and sport as part of the curriculum. Young ladies' exercise in mid-Victorian times had tended to be limited to the sedate 'crocodile walk' (girls processing along pavements two by two, in line) in order to take the air. The growing popularity of Swedish gymnastics required light, unobtrusive clothing. Feminine fashions at that time notoriously restricted the body: skirts were long and heavy, blouses elaborate and tight. Corsets and stiff stays made free movement impossible. Miss Buss deplored the fashion for tight lacing and tiny waists, and encouraged simple, loose clothing in the gym.

Miss Buss's arrangements at the North London Collegiate were often taken as a model for the high schools for girls which were founded across the country in the late nineteenth and early twentieth centuries, and in particular for the schools established by the Girls Public Day School Company and the newer state or municipal grammar schools that followed. There was a general trend for uniforms to be introduced by way of the need for clothing suitable for physical education. Gradually, the light tunics worn for games or in the gym came to be seen as suitable daywear. By the 1900s, a few of the more elite girls' schools (Roedean, Downe House) had settled on girls wearing a loose tunic called a *djibbah* as a form of uniform. This garment was allegedly inspired by African tribal costume. It was knee-length, hung from the shoulder with a 'T' shaped insert at the neck, and was worn over a loose blouse. At Roedean the girls wore a *djibbah* in plain material during the day, but changed into a fancier version, with velvet inserts or an arty embroidered yoke, for the evening. But the garment which really caught on as a staple of girls' school uniform at this time was of course the gymslip.

The gymslip is generally credited to have been designed in the early 1890s. Gymslips were usually in serge or gaberdine, they hung from the shoulders, and were square-necked, knee-length tunics. Some had box pleats. If the wearer had breasts, they flattened the chest. The shirt and tie commonly worn underneath would have a similar effect. There was often a girdle to go with the gymslip, sometimes woven in 'house' or team colours. In the 1920s this would be worn low on the hips, in the 1950s it was more likely to circle the waist. Accessorised with a hockey stick, the gymslip unambiguously denoted 'schoolgirl'.

The gymslip was widely adopted by girls' schools across the country in the 1920s. By this time, the idea of physical exercise for girls was losing some of its contentiousness, although some still argued that competitive sports were unfeminine and a threat to the establishment of a healthy menstrual cycle. But most girls' schools had come to regard physical education as an essential part of the curriculum. As the gymslip passed from games into daywear, physical education moved towards requiring even more radical outfitting: shorts, divided skirts, short-sleeved Aertex blouses and the like. By the 1920s and 1930s, the gymslip was no longer out of keeping with general fashion trends: short 'flapper'-type dresses with dropped waistlines were worn by most young women in those decades.

The same decades saw an explosion in the popularity of the girls' school story. Writers such as Angela Brazil, Elsie Oxenham, Dorita Fairlie Bruce and Elinor Brent-Dyer inspired generations of schoolgirls with stories of adventure, pluck and camaraderie. Both the First and the Second World Wars generated enthusiasm for the wearing of uniform as a mark of patriotism and this fed back into the growing acceptance of uniform regulations in schools in peacetime.

This idea of uniform as an expression of *esprit de corps* and youthful citizenship was apparent in the youth movements of the early twentieth century, in particular in Scouting and Guiding. Before then, the most prominent youth organisation for girls was the Girls' Friendly Society, the 'uniform' of which was limited to the wearing of white dresses and communion veils to indicate purity. The GFS took a strong line on purity from the outset: non-virgins, even if penitent, were regarded as ineligible for membership until the rule was relaxed in the 1930s.

In contrast to this, Guiding was about adventure, though not of course the sexual kind. The story goes that when Baden-Powell turned up to inspect Boy Scouts at the movement's first official rally at the Crystal Palace in 1909, he was somewhat put out to find a party of girls calling themselves Girl Scouts and demanding inspection along with the boys. Anxious to keep Scouting a manly preserve, Baden-Powell insisted that the girls form a separate movement (Girl Guides rather than Girl Scouts) which wouldn't look too 'unwomanly'. B-P's sister, Agnes, took charge for a while, suppressing some of the more mettlesome patrol names chosen by the girls themselves ('wildcats', 'wolves', 'ravens', etc.), in favour of more discreetly feminine appellations ('roses', 'cornflowers' and 'lilies'). The more enthusiastic attempts to emulate the boys' uniforms (stout poles, Scout belts and haversacks, short skirts over bare knees) were also toned down. Guides were instructed to wear skirts (ankle length), with knickers and stockings in dark blue. Nevertheless, many girls found the uniform an inspiration: liberating (no petticoats, white haversacks, sensible boots), and took great pride in its elements of quasi-martial decoration (white ties and shoulder knots, lanyard and knife, and in some cases, large hats with bunches of cock's plumes at the side). Contemporary accounts show that there was no shortage of controversy over such garb. One early Guide reported that 'many mothers refused to let their girls "run the streets" in uniform', and that 'the old ladies in the parish' voiced their disgust 'in no uncertain terms': 'we were an excellent target, not only for verbal abuse from the roughs in the neighbourhood, but for the throwing of stones and tomatoes that had seen better days'.

By the end of the 1914–18 war such controversy abated: Guides had been enthusiastically drawn into the war effort in many ways and had established a reputation for stalwart patriotism. Uniforms for women no longer looked so new-fangled. In 1937, the young Princess Elizabeth was registered as a Guide, her sister Margaret, a Brownie. Their mother also joined the Girl Guides' Association, and the first Buckingham Palace Guide Company was set up so that the young princesses could start earning their challenge badges. The Second World War further accentuated the idea of girls' uniform as indicative of loyalty to the Crown and patriotism. In 1944 the British public was treated to a Pathé newsreel film feature showing Princess Elizabeth (in the uniform of a Sea Ranger) and her sister Margaret Rose (in Guide uniform) having a wonderful time hopping in and out of trenches, with Margaret helping with camp cooking ('a ration of lettuce carried away in regulation mess tins'), while their mum, and Crackers the corgi, looked on.

My mother always regarded herself as a contemporary of the Princess Elizabeth, some aspects of their lives (girlhood, marriage, children) running in parallel, although sadly, my mother didn't live anything like so long as the late Queen. I have a photo of Mum looking young and fresh-faced, dressed in the uniform of the Women's Junior Air Corps (WJAC),

CHAPTER THREE

My mother, Connie, resplendent in her
Women's Junior Air Corps uniform, early 1940s

sometime around 1943. It's a studio portrait, and I'm sure she was proud of the way she looked, in her light grey jacket, shirt and tie, her hair rolled into glossy coils and tucked neatly under the grey, buttoned cap, on which you can just glimpse the triangular WJAC badge. Young women had been keen to join the cadet forces in wartime, but it wasn't until 1940 that the government instructed Florence Horsburgh, the then Minister for Education, to set up the National Association of Training Corps for Girls. The WJAC came under this umbrella and girls flocked to join. They were taught Morse and semaphore, how to change fuses and washers, and how to recognise different kinds of aircraft. Some collected milk bottle tops or rosehips (for vitamin additives) to aid in the war effort. The government was a bit halfhearted about all this. But Mum spoke with great enthusiasm about her experience.

The postwar years saw many, if not most, girls accustomed to some kind of uniform, either through membership of youth organisations, or as an accepted part of schooling. School stories were widely read, and new magazines and comics featuring schoolgirl adventures and representing an idealised version of boarding-school life circulated widely. Stories of pluck and daring in *School Friend* and *Girls' Crystal* thrilled a whole generation of girls, and this literature undoubtedly conduced to the popular acceptance of uniform.

But things were changing. Parodies proliferated: the girls' school story was the butt of well-aimed satire but also gentle, affectionate humour in the writings of Arthur Marshall (*Girls will be Girls*, *Giggling in the Shrubbery*). Schoolgirls themselves were represented as subversive little horrors in Ronald Searle's massively popular St Trinian's cartoons and in the series of films inspired by his drawings. Searle's lumpy little anarchists drank, smoked, and were full of ghoulish schemes and violent intent. His sixth formers were sexually aware, bursting out of their blouses and gymslips, bent on experience and seduction.

Girls dressed in uniforms once designed for modesty became the focus for all kinds of masculine projection: most of these representations of schoolgirls were the work of men. They might be well received by women, though, precisely *because* of their subversiveness: it was a relief to get away from stifling prescriptions for feminine modesty. Cartoonist Posy Simmonds has written about how as a seven-year-old she came across Searle's St Trinian's drawings as revelatory: girls didn't have to be goody-goody, 'soppy, drippy and utterly wet'; they could scheme and plot and misbehave, just like boys. By the 1960s, though, school uniform had become increasingly fetishised, especially in certain kinds of pulp literature with its many luridly erotic tales of discipline and punishment, often centring on reform school girls.

With the extension of secondary education to all in postwar Britain, a new generation of girls went through school regarding education more as a right than a privilege. These girls were increasingly articulate critics of the systems of discipline and regulation to which they were subjected. In the autobiographical accounts of educational experience published by anthropologist Judith Okely, who attended a girls' public boarding school in the 1950s, or sociologist Mary Evans, a grammar school girl of similar vintage, girls' schooling, with its finickity dress codes and uniform regulations, both reflected and reproduced the endless contradictions inherent in expectations of femininity at the time. Girls were expected to work and study hard, whilst ambitions for careers were vague or nonexistent. Sexual awareness, or any interest in adorning the body, was routinely repressed. Many teachers remained unmarried, and girls and parents often pitied them, judging the making of an advantageous marriage a prime feminine goal.

Expectations around social class were less conflicted than those around femininity. Judith Okely's school catered for a privileged elite of girls, some of whom would have been expected to go on to finishing school, or as young debs, to 'come out' and display themselves on the social scene in order to lure a rich husband. What was in store for bright grammar school girls was much less clear. The autobiographies of grammar school girls usually record passing the eleven-plus as a key event in their lives, to be followed by the major *rite de passage* of securing the appropriate school uniform. For girls from less than prosperous homes, this could involve serious anxiety. Girls awarded grammar school places sometimes declined them on the grounds that their parents simply couldn't afford the uniform. In the memoir of her childhood, *A Green Girl*, sociologist Phyllis Willmott recalled that her mother had wanted her to decline the place she had been awarded at the John Roan School in Greenwich in the 1930s because of the formidable cost of the uniform. Phyllis's near contemporary, Rose Gamble, another London girl who passed the scholarship and was offered a place at a secondary school in the 1930s, similarly recorded her family's horror at being presented with the uniform list, 'lisle stockings were for ladies' and 'the gymslip alone cost more than Mum's wages for a week'.

Phyllis Willmott, like Rose Gamble, remembered the valiant efforts her parents and family had made to keep costs down: trying to source replica items of uniform in Marks and Spencer, or the cheaper department stores. There was often resort to home dressmaking, or an attempt to find stuff second-hand. The trouble was, grammar school uniforms were expensive precisely because they spelled 'middle-class': official lists of innumerable items were supplied by posh outfitters. There were blazers and crests, shoe bags and science overalls, often indoor and outdoor shoes, Panamas and velour hats depending on the season. It could cost a fortune. Not having the 'right' pullover, or wearing a lumpy home-knitted one, could spell terrible anxiety, because one's peers would *know* and might judge accordingly. The argument that school uniform was a

CHAPTER THREE

John Bull cover image from the 1950s showing the gulf between school uniform and fashionable femininity

leveller, a promotor of social equality, was as threadbare as that about there being 'parity of esteem' between grammar schools and secondary modern schools: it simply didn't wash.

Late in 2021, the UK government seemed to have come round to realising this. In November that year it issued statutory guidance urging schools to think twice about uniform regulations: to avoid branded items from single contract suppliers and to make every attempt to ensure that parents did not have to think about the cost of uniform when selecting a school for their offspring. But this only applied, of course, to the state system. So it may be considered something of a missed goal.

FOUR

Sex Kitten, Beat Girl

THE *OXFORD ENGLISH DICTIONARY* gives 1958 for an early use of the term 'sex kitten', used to describe, of course, Brigitte Bardot. Bardot's style, mid-last century, was unmistakeable. Her clothes were casual, sexy, *chic*. Cropped Capri pants, worn with Repetto ballerina flats. Off-the-shoulder sundresses, gingham with broderie anglaise trim. Eyeliner with cat-flicks at the corner, luxuriant cascades of tousled blonde hair. And more than the clothes and make-up, the way she walked and danced and held herself, the subtle insouciance, the pout, suggestive of a desire to please or appease no-one, particularly, apart from herself. Bardot's unmistakeable sex-kitten look has proved unforgettable too, regularly inspiring fashion columns down to the present day.

The term 'sex kitten' sounds at least mildly offensive, though, and certainly silly, today. It was the product of male representation and desires, as the *OED* entry recognised, quoting the *Daily Sketch* use of the term in a comment about Bardot to the effect that 'clever film men have moulded her sex-kitten type'.

Roger Vadim was regularly credited with having created the Bardot legend, the first in a line of such 'discoveries' or 'creations'; women whom he married or lived with and who were destined for stardom, Bardot's successors being Annette

 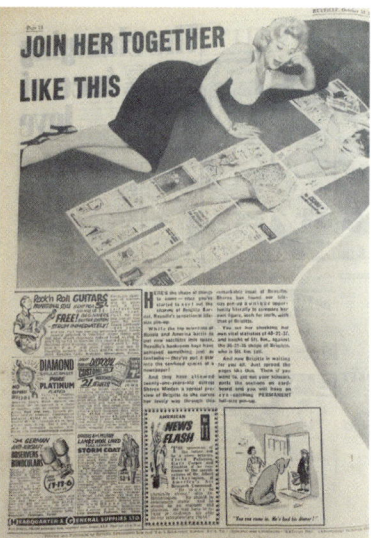

Reveille's cut-and-paste Bardot, October 1957

Stroyberg, Catherine Deneuve and Jane Fonda. Bardot had the biggest impact of all, becoming a legend in her own lifetime: indeed, she was already legendary, engendering a kind of cult, by the time she was in her mid-twenties.

The British press was enthralled by Bardot. In 1957 the popular paper *Reveille* advertised a life-size reproduction of her shapely body, printed over four or five pages. You had to cut out the pages and assemble her like a kind of wall chart. (Today, elderly men, teenage boys at the time, remember this pin-up fondly. Artist Peter Blake drew upon the image, surrounding it with cutlery, to produce a piece of pop art suggesting a knife thrower's board or act at the circus.) The prose used by male journalists to describe Bardot's charms in the late 1950s and early 1960s was often glutinous and cringeworthy. Alan Dent, in the *Illustrated London News*, dubbed her 'the last word in fondlesome kittens'. The *Daily Mirror*'s Donald Zec reported that Bardot had been sighted on a luxury yacht with Raoul Lévy, producer of the film *And God Created Woman* (1956),

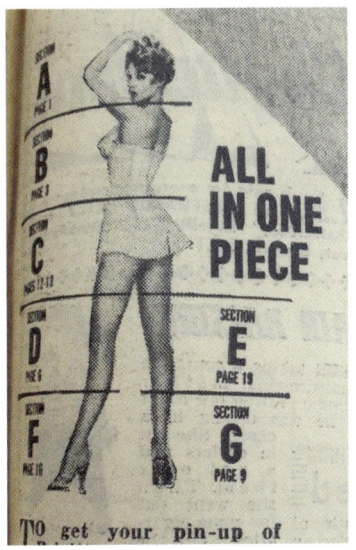
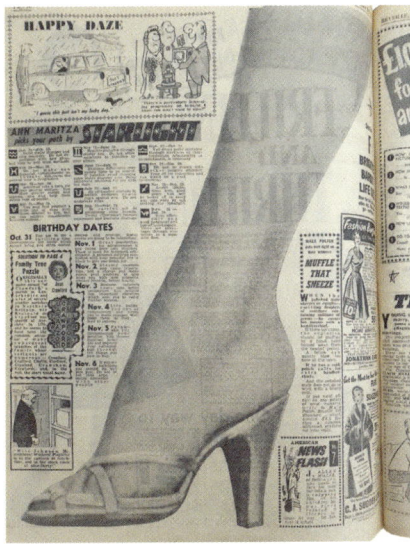

who 'also owns and steers a curvy little craft with crafty little curves name of Brigitte "The Sex Kitten" Bardot'. There was a great deal of drooling over sultriness, pouts and wiggling, punctuated on rare occasions by some attempt to consider Bardot's reaction to all the media exposure and the costs of fame. In an editorial comment entitled 'The Vamp and the Kitten' (26 October 1963), the *Daily Mail* showed itself a bit more reflective. Taking Marlene Dietrich as a prototype of the vamp, the writer suggested that she intimidated men. Bardot, childlike, flattered them into thinking themselves all-powerful, opining that 'The Bardot cult must have set women's notions of themselves back by a hundred years.'

Given all this, it's surprising to come across Simone de Beauvoir's essay on 'Brigitte Bardot and the Lolita Syndrome', originally written for the men's magazine *Esquire* in 1959. This was written ten years after de Beauvoir's ground-breaking and magisterial feminist text, *The Second Sex*. The *Esquire* essay is regularly cited as acclaiming Bardot a 'locomotive of women's history', or as seeing her as 'the first liberated woman of post-war France'. Leaving aside for the moment the question of linking Bardot with the fictional Lolita (who was twelve years old at the beginning of Nabokov's novel, fourteen at the end), de Beauvoir's analysis is perplexing for contemporary feminism. After all, Bardot's career was disturbing, coloured by sexploitation and episodes of depression, anguish and several attempts at suicide.

So why did de Beauvoir see her as a new kind of woman? I think there are at least two important insights here. The first concerns de Beauvoir's perception of Bardot as having sexual agency and appetite: her status as a sexual being with desires of her own. 'In love,' insisted de Beauvoir, Bardot 'was a hunter as much as prey'. Men are an object for her, as much as she is an object for them. She was careful to note the distinction between representations and reality, and a modern feminist might be more ambivalent in judging here, but Bardot's demeanour suggested sexual autonomy rather than a steady desire to please. 'This is precisely what hurts male pride,' de Beauvoir added. Her second insight, allied to the first, concerned Bardot's rejection of 'kept woman' status. Her style was devoid of artifice, de Beauvoir wrote, 'she goes about barefooted, she turns up her nose at elegant clothes, jewels, girdles, perfumes, make-up'. It was this indifference that could be unnerving, she contended:

> In the Latin countries, where men cling to the myth of 'the woman as object', BB's naturalness seems to them more perverse than any possible sophistication. To spurn jewels and cosmetics and high heels and girdles is to refuse to transform oneself into a remote idol. It is to assert that one is man's fellow and equal, to recognise that between the woman and him there is mutual desire and pleasure.

In essence, de Beauvoir saw Bardot's style as a rejection of anything suggesting the trophy woman. In a culture where conservative ideas of the male provider and the bourgeois family reigned strong, and which sought to contain female sexuality within these structures, Bardot's style could look subversive. Like the heroine of *And God Created Woman*, she might break out and act untamed, and she just didn't care. French journalist Agnès Poirier recorded a story told by Louis Malle, filming with Bardot in a shopping arcade in Lausanne. A woman in a fur coat came up to Brigitte while she was acting, spat full in her face and screamed 'You are undermining the bourgeoisie.'

Writers in the British press were keen to find a homegrown equivalent to Bardot. According to the *Daily Mail*, the most successful contender was a fourteen-year-old called Gillian Hills, allegedly sighted by Roger Vadim in Nice. Gillian was described as the 'English Sex Kitten', 'pouting' for the camera and as liberally 'flashing sultry glances right and left'. Hills' mother was reported as having encouraged her daughter to leave school: she was of the opinion that movie fame would be 'better than being a typist or a clerk in a post office'. Gillian was said to be missing friends of her own age and she was quoted as having complained that 'sometimes I feel I was in a zoo, with everybody looking at me'. It didn't stop her from feeling acutely disappointed when she was thought to be too young to star in Vadim's projected film, *Dangerous Liaisons*. Instead, at fifteen, she was cast in the role of Jennifer, a teenage daughter from hell in the 1960 British film *Beat Girl*, directed by Edmond T. Greville.

Gillian Hills as Beat Girl epitomises the Bardot look: cigarette pants, peasant blouses, ballerina pumps. A memorable banded full skirt, tightly belted; cascades of tousled blonde hair. Echoing Bardot in *And God Created Woman*, she dances like a maenad, as if in a trance, oblivious to all except her own body and the music. Jennifer's alienation from her bourgeois father and young French stepmother combines with potent teenage angst to drive her to the edge, into more and more forms of extreme anti-social behaviour: wild parties, daredevil driving escapades, the possibilities of performance as a stripper. The film's shaky narrative is about the last-minute rescue of this character: Jennifer is pulled back from the brink by family love and loyalty. *Beat Girl* sensationalises what the 1950s called 'Vice' (the world of 'Off Beat' music clubs and strip joints in darkest Soho), representing women as potential victims, slithering about on the edge of this seedy world. Both Jennifer and her stepmother, Nichole, are shored up against ruin by the benign face of patriarchy, the protection of Jennifer's rich dad.

Bardot's image as erotic hoyden – the long hair, split skirt, the ballet pumps or barefoot abandon – fed into what was increasingly read as subversive 'Bohemian', even as 'beatnik', style. French singer Juliette Greco's image was another element in this, dark hair this time, and skinny black sweaters, but similar informality and cat-flick eyeliner. The late 1950s and 1960s were a time when the new independence of teenage daughters looked threatening to 'respectable' family life and values. There was widespread anxiety about girls getting pregnant outside marriage, which would bring shame and stigma on the family. Traditional patterns of courtship monitored (if not controlled) by parents were breaking down, eroded by the force of the Teenage Revolution. For many, in this context, beatnik style was a warning of *subversion*.

A short film produced by British Pathé in 1963, entitled *Beatnik Beauty*, might be read as an attempt to tame girls through style. In London's West End we are introduced to Stephanie Beaumont, who dresses like a beatnik, the commentary tells us. To a present day viewer she looks cool and relaxed, wearing a black sweater with a pendant, jeans and a leather jacket. Stephanie is hauled into a posh Mayfair beauty salon where two white-coated lady beauticians with tortured bouffant hair-dos take her in hand, subjecting her to egg rinses, hair rollers, anti-wrinkle treatments and face masks. When she emerges, she is overly groomed, stiff and lacquered, encased in tight brocade and lamé. The commentator burbles delight in what he sees as her elegance and a Cinderella-type transformation; to us she looks much older and defeated: kept woman rather than free spirit.

But fewer younger women were finding themselves drawn to this style of formal, manicured elegance. Fur coats and crocodile handbags were beginning to look dated. When Bardot married Jacques Charrier in June 1959, she had broken with tradition to wear a full-skirted, button-through dress in sugar-pink gingham check, trimmed at elbow and neck with white broderie anglaise. Her hair was left loose. She looked sensational. Four years later, Barbara Hulanicki and her new husband Stephen Fitz-Simon were contemplating setting up a mail-order fashion business, which they decided to call Biba. Felicity Green, fashion editor of the *Daily Mirror*, suggested they work together on a feature about career girls, and that Barbara should design a dress which readers could order. Hulanicki decided on a pink gingham minidress with a keyhole opening at the back and a matching Bardot-style kerchief. The new Biba dress, which cost 25 shillings, received over 17,000 orders.

FIVE

Baby Dolls and Dollybirds

ALISON SETTLE'S COLUMN IN the *Observer* in February 1958 was headed 'This Frightening Passion for Childhood's Look'. Settle was reporting on the spring collections, newly exhibited in Paris. Several designers were showing some kind of youthful look, she announced, though she was careful to draw fine distinctions. St Laurent 'had introduced a deliberately childish simplicity' into some coats and dresses, but he had not 'fallen into the error of turning women into dolls and babies', she judged, 'as have various other designers'. Guy Laroche had shown dresses falling from the shoulder, 'in wide box pleats slotted with loose girdles like school tunics', but 'these, too, are not doll clothes', she opined. Givenchy, similarly, had come up with plenty of 'little girl' styles. But Jacques Griffe, in her opinion, went too far:

> [He] kills the theme with pleated 'Baby Doll' chemises that swing from décolleté to unbroken hem, for all hours of the day, from wools to chiffon. It is the rising of the skirt line to as much as 19 inches off the ground that has brought out this frightening passion for childhood's look.

What did Settle find so 'frightening' here? Was she thinking about Nabokov's *Lolita,* perhaps, published in France a few years earlier, in 1955? The book was originally banned in Britain. But Graham Greene's enthusiastic review of *Lolita* in the *Sunday Times* that year did much to stimulate discussion and controversy, as did John Gordon's proclamation in the *Sunday Express* that it constituted 'the filthiest book' he had ever read. The eagerly anticipated first British edition of *Lolita* was to be published by Weidenfeld and Nicolson in 1959. Settle was closely associated with literary circles, and will have known about this. The word 'nymphet', rare before it was coined by Nabokov to refer to 'bewitching maidens' between the ages of nine and fourteen, had entered popular discourse. It may be, further, that Settle was thinking of Tennessee Williams' screenplay for the film *Baby Doll* (1956), starring Carroll Baker in its title role. Though nineteen years old, Baby Doll Meighan is a virgin, an immature child-bride who sucks her thumb and sleeps in a crib. When she experiences a sexual awakening, it is not with her husband. The film did much to popularise the term 'baby doll' as a description of a short slip, gown or nightdress, often – in the case of nightwear – sheer and revealing, with ruffled neckline and pants.

Questions around adolescent sexuality were much in the air, not least because of these cultural productions. Girls were marrying earlier and earlier after the Second World War: teenage brides were commonplace, but the trend towards youthful marriage was nonetheless a cause of concern to many. Where were the boundaries? As discussed in the previous chapter, when Bardot lookalike Gillian Hills left school at fourteen to pursue a film career her decision attracted decidedly negative comments in the popular press. 'Is Doing a Bardot Fair to a 14-Year-Old Schoolgirl?' asked Paul Tanfield in the *Daily Mail*.

Was Alison Settle disapproving of 'baby-doll' clothing and very short skirts because she objected to the sexual objectification of young girls? Did she see these fashions as infantilising women? Or was her dislike based more on grounds of taste? There can be little doubt that her own sartorial preferences were for the elegant, the classily chic, the restrained. In a collection of her essays on fashion, brought together and re-published in a volume entitled *Clothes Line* in 1937, Settle was stern against 'overdoing things': 'resist all tendency to fluffiness', she abjured, insisting that 'showiness is the deathblow to fine dressing'.

Settle was ambivalent about teenage fashion. As early as 1956 she noted the incongruity of being driven across Paris to a celebratory launch of a new perfume by Mme Carven by a blonde woman cab driver with her hair in a ponytail ('horsetail hair-do'), wearing duffel coat and jeans. While she was always pleased to note expanding opportunities for women, she valued *couture* and elite culture. Taste in gloves and handbags she saw as connoisseurship, akin to knowing about fine wines. She made sharp comments about American buyers catering for what she labelled 'the youth kick', and street fashion, for her, edged towards vulgarity. It is hard to see her looking upon baby-doll nighties or miniskirts without a shudder.

The 'baby-doll look' nevertheless took hold fast. A photograph of women modelling Valerie Evans designs at a spring lingerie show in London in 1957 features a line-up of grown women with coiffured, set hair, in transparent, frilly, baby-doll nightwear, one clutching an actual child's doll; underneath the sheer fabric they wear sturdy, figure-controlling underwear. To modern eyes they look ridiculous. Fashion journalist Phyllis Heathcote, like Alison Settle, found the trend ludicrous, and wrote an article for the *Guardian* in 1958 saying so. The *Oxford English Dictionary* gives as an early example of usage of the term 'baby doll' an article in the *Spectator* reporting from the Venice Film Festival in 1959, the author observing the ubiquity of young girls clad in '"baby doll" outfits' with 'the nymphet look which has been in fashion this summer', adding tartly that 'behind their dark

CHAPTER FIVE

Designer Valerie Evans introducing her 1957 baby-doll nightwear

glasses they were very big girls indeed'. The advertisement sections of popular newspapers such as *Reveille* offered a wide range of cheap, synthetic baby-doll nighties. But whilst mature women may have been influenced by the fashion, the look really belonged to the young. The 'baby doll' segued into the 'dollybird': slim, often long-haired and round eyed, typically wearing a miniskirt.

In her 1959 essay on 'Brigitte Bardot and the Lolita Syndrome', discussed in the previous chapter, Simone de Beauvoir mused on contemporary interest in 'the child-woman'. She suggested that writers and film producers (who she called 'the dream merchants') had 'created a new Eve' by merging the 'green fruit' and *'femme fatale'*. The appeal of the child-woman was hardly new: the German term *backfisch*, for instance, had long been used to suggest the attractiveness of the adolescent girl on the cusp of maturity. But de Beauvoir's contention that this appeal of the child-woman, to men, had been intensified by progress towards equality between the sexes in the modern world, was perceptive. 'In an age when woman drives a car and speculates on the stock exchange,' she considered, the age difference between an adult man and a very young woman 're-establishes the distance between them that seems necessary to desire'. This went some way towards explaining the postwar interest in erotic hoydens or nymphets, she thought: it pandered to the male ego in making men feel safer about, and less challenged by women. It didn't always work, of course. It is worth remembering that Tennessee Williams' Baby Doll Meighan challenges and slips out of her husband's control. Lolita escapes the clutches of creepy Humbert. And Bardot eventually declared that, having given her beauty and her youth to men, she would devote her wisdom and experience to animal welfare.

Baby dolls, dollybirds: were these epithets and the styles associated with them altogether demeaning of women? Feminists recoil from such language today, but language and representations need to be understood in context. We associate the dollybird with Swinging London, with the Youthquake and the Teenage Revolution. All of these could be argued to have unsettled conventional gender stereotypes, and to have constituted stepping stones – however slippery and insecure – to 'liberation'. If it is hard to think of 'little girl' styles as liberating, it is equally hard to see – say – the youthful fashions developed by Mary Quant, Barbara Hulanicki and other designers of the clothes sold in the plethora of new boutiques which blossomed in the 1960s as wholly oppressive or demeaning to women. There was a great deal of ambiguity in and around these sixties and seventies fashions, not surprising at this time of rapid social change.

The flowering of boutiques and street fashion challenged the hegemony of Paris and *haute couture*, reflecting and stimulating changing patterns of consumption. Young people had greater spending power than before the war, and as studies such as that of sociologist Mark Abrams reported, teenage girls were spending a large proportion of their income on clothes and cosmetics. Abrams estimated that in 1959, 'the average girl' spent over a £1 a week on clothes, shoes and make-up. The teenage market, he submitted, was almost entirely working class, since many of the middle-class youngsters were still at school. But others saw potential here. Even those teenage girls still at school no longer wanted to dress like their mothers, and many of these would have had disposable income through pocket money, dress allowances or their own Saturday or part-time jobs. And the period between leaving school and getting married was often one of intense preoccupation with appearance. When Audrey Slaughter founded *Honey* magazine in 1960, it was this kind of market she had in mind.

To stride out in a high street chain-store version of Courrèges boots and miniskirt felt a lot more liberated than struggling into an elasticated panty-girdle hung with rubbery suspenders, fine denier stockings and crippling high heels. Contemporaries often remarked on the air of independence that surrounded the dollybird, 'Biba' or 'Chelsea girl'. Barbara Hulanicki remembered the classic Biba girl as looking sweet, but 'as hard as nails': 'She did what she felt like at that moment and had no Mum to influence her judgement.' Where mothers had once advised on clothes and style, the peer group and teenage magazines now stepped in to guide fashion choices. Magazines such as *Honey* and *Petticoat* weren't interested in rules about dressing involving respectability, gloves and hats: instead, they represented fashion choices as *fun*.

There can be a touch of wide-eyed vacancy in the expression on models' faces in the fashion photography of the sixties and early seventies, a caught-in-the-headlights look. Young women may have appeared bold and independent to their parents and elders, but there was a vulnerability too, in part no doubt because of the very speed of change. Teenage girls were often uncertain about what they wanted, not least because it wasn't altogether clear what their options were. Educational, occupational and contraceptive choices were opening up, but still limited. The advent of the pill made new forms of sexual behaviour possible, but getting hold of it wasn't always straightforward. Even when it was freely available, girls might be uneasy about looking too experienced or prepared in sexual matters: innocence was still associated with femininity.

Did young women always want freedom from male 'protection'? Such freedom raised difficult issues in a still unequal society. It often made sense to hedge one's bets. And ambivalence surely entered into fashion choices. In her paper, 'Womanliness as Masquerade', written in 1928–29, psychoanalyst Joan Rivière suggested that women might use femininity as a mask to lessen anxiety and any fear of retribution consequent upon their showing rivalry with men. An ambitious young woman at university in the 1960s may well have felt comfortable being described as a 'dollybird' and wearing pretty, feminine 'Dollyrockers by Sambo' dresses. Wearing garments like this was more acceptable in some institutions and workplaces than less conventionally ladylike trouser suits and brogues.

More and more girls were setting their sights on university in Britain in the 1960s. University prospectuses – particularly those of the 'new' universities of the 1960s such as East Anglia, Keele and Sussex – capitalised on this. Their prospectuses began to feature photographs of attractive, miniskirted young women talking animatedly in common rooms and on library steps. The photos were designed to make university life look *fun*, to attract men of course, as well as women. The 'dollybird' effectively became both a lure and a branding image for the new, modern university. This was a big social change.

The image of a university student earlier in the century had usually been one of a bespectacled 'Varsity' man, clad in tweeds and probably smoking a pipe. Only about a quarter of the student body had been female in the 1950s, and in some universities, they were expected to stay in the background, to dress demurely and in a ladylike fashion, even discouraged from wearing 'slacks' or trousers.

A fashion feature focusing on women students in the October 1966 issue of *Honey* magazine gives insights into contemporary attitudes. The editor introduced the feature with mock apprehension: when planning campus visits, we are told, the photographic team wondered what they would find. Would women students be scary? Like 'a race of fierce cannibals'? Would they be too serious-minded to be interested in fashion, frivolity and glitter? But no, they were pleased to report that the female student could appear quite normal, and as interested in clothes and make-up as any other girl. Girl students from Cambridge, Keele, Leeds and Aberystwyth were photographed in a variety of trendy clothes. There were crepe 'babydoll' dresses, 'suede dolly-shoes', hairpieces, false eyelashes and fun-furs; also cowboy shirts and combat jackets, and a trouser suit with 'a lean, mean jacket and aggressive lapels'. The impression given was one of fashion opening up, of a whole new world of styles and possibilities for women. The article was entitled 'The Brain Bunnies'.

Impossible though it is not to cringe at the term 'Brain Bunny' today, it reminds us yet again that even in the sixties, the idea of a young woman having both a brain and an attractive body, or an interest in fashion, could appear challenging. Debates over the desirability of higher education for girls still tended to polarise women into two categories, 'career women' (bespectacled, swotty, unattractive) and 'normal women' bent on marrying at an early age and securing a home and family. 'The mind-body problem of an intellectual woman in the

Advert for Bri-Nylon, 1960s

1950s was… one of rigorous conflict,' wrote novelist Antonia Byatt, thinking back to her years at university. The body required sex and childbearing, and 'quite likely the death of the mind'. She remembered one of her woman tutors being so high-minded that she thought that women scholars should stay celibate. In *Sex Kittens Go to College*, an American comedy film produced in 1960, college life is thrown into total disarray when a computer chooses a highly educated woman as a head of science. She's presented as brilliant, but has a beautiful body and once worked as a stripper. It's a deplorably bad film, but reminds us that the idea of a desirable woman having a good brain was, even in quite recent history, a reliable staple of farce.

These assumptions help in part to explain why fashion, during this turbulent period of social history, came up with some strange ideas. Styles of dress were often full of ambiguity. *Honey* and other magazines catering for young women regularly featured adverts for clothes in new synthetic materials such as Courtelle, Orlon and Bri-Nylon. A series of adverts for Bri-Nylon riffed on the theme of 'Breakaway Girls'. It celebrated women embarking upon tasks in a new spirit of adventure. One such advert featured a young woman up a scaffold wearing a hard-hat. She's also wearing a flimsy, ruffled chemise and matching knickers: effectively a baby-doll nightie. Contradictions in fashion, bound up with different and challenging ideas about femininity, could be fought out on the body.

SIX

Classy Looks

WHAT ARE WE TO UNDERSTAND BY 'classy' dressing? The *Oxford English Dictionary* defines 'classy' as meaning 'of high or superior social class; *esp.* stylish and sophisticated'. If we turn to the internet, there are any number of contemporary websites which set out to enlighten us about the principles of classy dressing. Words like 'sophistication' and 'elegance' predominate: descriptions of tailored, form-fitting garments in expensive natural fabrics (linen, cashmere, silk) abound. Classy dressing is also commonly defined in terms of what it is *not*: the advice is generally to look modest, to avoid the overtly sexy, overly short skirts, cheap synthetic fabrics, too much cleavage, the bare midriff. Jewellery should not be too elaborate or showy, it's a good idea to go for 'one good pair of pearl stud earrings'. Classy dressing is regularly held to be 'timeless' or 'classic'.

It is hard to see how fashions and viewpoints can ever be 'timeless'. Alison Settle, whose personal taste rarely strayed from an ideal of restrained elegance, often made fashion statements that were inflected by social class. She insisted, for instance, that the best-dressed women were often those of moderate or limited income, because being more budget-conscious, they had to think more clearly before purchasing clothes. Rich women might be more inclined to 'vulgarity', she explained:

CHAPTER SIX

> Be deeply thankful if you are not a rich woman: such seem hardly able to resist the lure of adding an unsuitable spray of orchids to an already rather over-trimmed dress, or, worse still, to a fur coat. Heaven forbid that you should ever be rich enough to endure the temptation to add orchids to fur, so making yourself look fussy, ugly, overdone.

Few women today are likely to be troubled by the vulgarity of adding orchids to fur. But even Settle's idea of a 'classic', classy fur coat has failed the test of time. Settle left *Vogue* in somewhat unhappy circumstances in 1935 (she was fired). But her ideals of restrained elegance lived on in the shape of *Vogue*'s 'Mrs Exeter', who appeared in the magazine's pages between 1948 and the 1960s. Mrs Exeter was a fictional character, a sophisticated, elegant lady of mature years: 'Approaching sixty, Mrs Exeter does not look a day younger, a fact she accepts with perfect good humour and reasonableness.' From 1954 she was modelled by the thirty-something-years-old Margot Smyly. The image was one of quality cut, good pearls, serviceable furs and quiet elegance. You could imagine her as one of the county set, wearing a black cocktail dress set off by a marcasite pheasant brooch, her shoulders warmed by a mink stole. Mrs Exeter was not over-rich, and cared about value for money, but she was very definitely upper middle, or solid middle class.

Girls growing up in the 1950s and 1960s learned that class and respectability were closely entwined. You had to avoid looking 'common'. There was shame involved in this, you didn't want to be labelled 'tarty' or 'cheap'. Girls who wanted 'to make something of themselves' had two routes: education or marriage to a man 'with prospects', or above them on the social scale. Education wasn't a fail-safe route to social mobility in the middle of the last century, because even if you did well in school and university, career openings for women were still very limited. Marriage was a better bet, and marrying up was more likely if you looked classy. Cinderella stories of women from humble origins marrying princes were extremely popular at this time. Even if you couldn't afford to dress well, you could somehow try to convey class through behaviour and comportment. Walt Disney's animated film version of Cinderella in 1950 was a massive success. A number of the films of the 1950s and 1960s are about class transformation facilitated through dress and deportment: *Sabrina Fair* (1954), *Gigi* (1958) and *My Fair Lady* (1964) all play with this theme.

For many girls in these years, Audrey Hepburn was a particular inspiration. In her films, she oozed class. Her dresses – particularly those designed by Hubert de Givenchy and Edith Head – are wonderful. In *Roman Holiday*, Hepburn plays the part of a princess who hankers after an escape from royal duties and goes absent without leave for a time in Rome. In spite of being drugged up and reduced to sleeping on the streets for a night, she keeps her white gloves on, and her classy and royal behaviour soon gives her away. *Sabrina Fair* stars Hepburn as a chauffeur's daughter sent to Paris to learn how to be a lady. She returns crafted into a vision of fashionable gorgeousness and ladylike grace, soon attracting the interest and devotion of her father's wealthy employer's son and heir. There are several memorable outfits and a particularly stunning, strapless, bare-shouldered, full-skirted, black-embroidered ballgown. Most iconic of all was the black cocktail dress Hepburn wore in *Breakfast at Tiffany's* (1961). It was worn with stranded pearls and a tiara-like diamanté hair ornament: Holly Golightly is a girl on the make, but Hepburn gives her unforgettable style and class. The tiara-like hair ornament, hinting at class privilege and entitlement (if not royalty), was widely copied.

Truman Capote, on whose novella *Breakfast at Tiffany's* (1958) the film was based, contended that Holly Golightly was not exactly a call girl, but more a representative of a new breed of girls who lived off, and took what they wanted from, well-off men. In his opinion she was more of an 'American geisha' figure. In the novella, there is no love affair between Holly and the protagonist, whereas in the film version the romance and suggestion of a happy-ever-after ending serve to redeem Holly from any accusation of being a real gold-digger. Similarly, Hepburn's achievement, in the film, is to combine and hence reconcile a kind of innocence and authenticity with worldly sophistication and bold self-interest. It's an unlikely combination, which she carries off with class.

Clothes play a major role in *Breakfast at Tiffany's*, as they do in most of the films in which Hepburn stars. One of the reasons why her style has had such enduring appeal, right down to the present day, is that in these films dress is used both to negotiate difficult social situations and to facilitate desired outcomes. You get what you want – and the man you want – by dressing in an inspired way. But Hepburn's style nonetheless incorporated an element of independence, even insouciance: she never *looked* on the make, desperate, overtly sexy or craven. She could look casual, wear capri pants with ballet shoes and a simple sweater as easily as a Givenchy ballgown and still manage somehow to suggest a kind of impeccable classiness.

Girls who went to fee-paying schools in the middle decades of the last century learned about class in a myriad of ways. Most important was what your father did, where his money came from, whether it was 'old' or 'new' money. Working on admissions in a 'new' university in the 1970s, I vividly recall reading a reference written by the headmistress of a well-known girls' public school which began by outlining the precise social status and family background of the girl candidate in question. Her own abilities were perceived as of less importance than her class position.

Girls in posh public schools might judge each other by the kind of car their parents drove to school events, how parents dressed, whether their mothers wore real or fake pearls, where families went on holiday. Something of this also went on in mainly middle-class grammar and high schools. There were clues to class in the newspapers one's parents read, the kind of house they lived in, their domestic arrangements, whether they ate 'dinner' at lunchtime or in the evening. A great deal of shame and embarrassment was often linked with these observations: girls could be cruel about the wearing of 'cheap' white shoes or second-hand clothes. And they could be cruel about their teachers, particularly if these teachers wore terrible clothes.

Female teachers in elite schools were sometimes hard to position in terms of social class, and they made uneasy or impossible role models. Whether through absent-mindedness, high-mindedness or for reasons of economy, they often seemed to go for mud-coloured, ill-fitting attire accessorised with baggy, pinky-brown stockings and sensible shoes. This, and the fact that many women teachers remained unmarried, tended to elicit condescension or even pity from their pupils. Some teachers retaliated with their own class-based threats: if girls didn't pay attention to their studies, they warned, 'they might end up working in Woolworths'.

The practice of sending girls to 'finishing school' in order to polish up their attractiveness to wealthy males prior to 'coming out' was waning in the late 1950s. Formal presentation of debutantes at Court ceased after 1958, not least because the system was perceived as failing to serve its main purpose of upholding social exclusivity. There were too many *nouveau riche* families keen to secure privilege for their daughters. Princess Margaret is said to have memorably declared that 'We had to put a stop to it. Every tart in London was getting in.'

In the context of rapid postwar social change, class markers were shifting. The Youthquake of the 1960s impacted seismically on the world of fashion. Looking back,

CHAPTER SIX

Fur, jewels and gloves: 'classy' femininity in 1950s

fashion writer Ernestine Carter recalled that 'The sixties began in deceptive quiet on the fashion front,' but that 'It was the quiet of a pan of milk about to boil.' Carter herself, who became associate editor of the *Sunday Times* in 1968, played a part in promoting the young designers associated with Swinging London. Fashionable trends began to blossom up from the street, rather than percolating down from Paris. Classiness and trendiness competed, and could become confused.

Vogue's grey-haired, elegant and classy Mrs Exeter can be seen as a casualty of the Youthquake. She was discontinued, abruptly, in 1964. *Vogue* archivist Robin Muir explains:

> *Vogue* replaced Mrs Exeter with 'Young Idea', Cecil Beaton with David Bailey… and the Hunt Ball in a draughty corn exchange with Swinging London happenings. Who wanted to be old? Not *Vogue*.

It wasn't just a case of slender, youthful Jean Shrimpton lookalikes replacing the well-groomed lady of the shires. There were deeper forces at stake. Women's aspirations were changing. Standards of female education had been rising since the Butler Education Act of 1944 and the expansion of universities in the 1960s. Young women were becoming more independent and developing ambitions beyond that of wifedom and motherhood. The goal of marrying as well and as soon as possible receded, at least for some, and the idea of being a 'kept woman' became less attractive. And that, after all, is what Mrs Exeter had represented. She existed on her husband's income, and her status, ultimately, depended on his.

Women's position in the class structure has always been complicated. For a long time, social scientists assumed that their class position derived from men. Daughters were positioned by fathers, until they married, when their social class derived from that of their husband. Such assumptions were never wholly satisfactory, and in the second half of the twentieth century they became even more questionable. With better education, the opening up of employment opportunities and more control over childbearing, women were increasingly able to fashion their own lives.

It is not altogether clear how much relevance traditional concepts of class have in twenty-first-century Britain. Measured objectively, class divisions remain strong and pervasive, and there is evidence of increasing inequalities of wealth. Opportunities for social mobility are often held to be declining. But although social theorists can classify people according to social and economic status, surveys show that nearly half the population are decidedly reluctant to identify themselves as members of any particular social class. The British Social Attitudes Survey concluded (in 2012) that since the 1980s, 'the salience of class has declined substantially for people'. Levels of income, education and type of occupation nonetheless continue to shape people's identities. But the hierarchy is no longer neat, complexities of status and identity politics cross through the layers.

In the early 1900s you could pretty much identify someone's social class from what they were wearing. Factory girls wore clogs and shawls, fisher girls a localised style of calico bonnets. After the First World War things became less clear, and writers such as George Orwell and J.B. Priestley commented on how the availability of mass-produced clothing and the influence of the cinema meant that factory girls could dress like actresses or film stars: you could no longer be sure of reading regional or social class status from what women wore. There was unease in this, as there was in the 1960s with the popularity of 'unisex' fashion: girls wearing trousers and boys sporting flowery shirts and wearing their hair long upset those observers who felt safer with traditional distinctions in place.

Unease about new money and traditional markers of gender and class can be seen in the sniggering attacks on 'Essex Girl' in the 1990s. This use of derision to bolster a sense of superiority and to allay unease fuelled many articles in the popular press, some of them ostensibly deploring the stereotype, but nevertheless retailing a clutch of misogynistic jokes. Essex girls were lampooned for their alleged promiscuity, but also for their taste: their short skirts, tight tops, bleach-highlighted hair and ostentatious gold jewellery, especially their alleged partiality for ankle-chains.

By the time the last century was drawing to a close, it had become increasingly difficult to identify what 'classy dressing' was: were 'designer' jeans classy? What about expensive handbags? Were clothes and footwear boasting brand names and designer labels to proclaim that they cost a lot classy or vulgar? Different social groups and subcultural groupings had their own rules of discrimination and fashion codes, but nothing reinforced identity quite so effectively as deriding other people's taste.

SEVEN

Power Dressing

IN 1977 JOHN T. MOLLOY, describing himself as 'America's best known clothing consultant', or alternatively, 'America's first wardrobe engineer', published *The Woman's Dress for Success Book*. It quickly became a bestseller. This 'was the most important book ever written about women's clothes', Molloy boasted, because it was based on scientific research rather than opinion. Most American women dressed for failure in the business world, he insisted. This was because they were too much influenced by the fashion industry, they dressed themselves as sex objects and they let their socio-economic background influence their choice of what to wear. If they wanted to improve their status in the workplace, they had to adopt a business uniform, in most cases the skirted suit and blouse was best. Sexiness wasn't a good idea because the more sexually attractive you looked, the less authoritative. However, you shouldn't try to dress like a man either because the 'imitation man look' put men off and backfired on you.

The book fired off a bewildering variety of dos and don'ts. 'Polyester pantsuits, sweaters, slacks, skirt and blouse outfits, and dresses with large prints all announce that you have no ambition,' decreed Molloy. 'Never wear lace when you want to exert authority,' was another shibboleth, and 'eyeliner is out'. Colours mattered. Purple, green and gold were all out, unless you were trying to attract an artist. Purple and gold, moreover, were lower-middle-class colours and therefore particularly dodgy. Don't have a flower on your desk, it's the badge of a secretary. Carry an attaché case not a handbag. If working in sales, you must 'dress richly', 'wield a gold pen', and 'you should drive a good car, preferably one that screams wealth – a sports car or a Mercedes is ideal'.

Molloy certainly understood something of women's dilemmas. 'Fashion for the woman lawyer is a time bomb,' he conceded. 'If she looks dated to women or chic to men, she will lose credibility.' It mattered whether the jury was black or white. If you were a black woman lawyer you had to dress very, very conservatively, except in circumstances where you were working with an urban black ghetto jury, in which case you might bend the rules to advantage. Thinking about all these directives must have made it difficult for serious followers of Molloy's dress rules to get out of bed in the morning. But his basic premise – that femininity in dress could undermine perceptions of authority – particularly in the gendered occupational world of the late twentieth century, held true.

This dilemma wasn't new. In the late nineteenth century, the first women who had sought to work in professional occupations, or in the public sphere more generally, had to be careful about what they wore. It was a double bind. To look too unfeminine might invite charges of mannishness or indiscretion, but to look authoritative meant avoiding looking too womanly. Women played the game the best they could. In the 1860s and 1870s, educational pioneer Emily Davies famously seated the prettiest and most becomingly dressed girl pupils at the front of the examination hall to avoid jibes about intellectual women looking unwomanly. Women academics sometimes affected a kind of late Victorian power dressing with collared shirt and tie under tightly tailored jackets over long skirts. The first generation of women dons in Oxford and Cambridge, denied academic dress, tended to invest in elaborate hats in an attempt to give themselves dignity. There's a well-known anecdote about classical scholar Hilda Lorimer, recorded in the Somerville College log book. In 1919, male students at Oriel broke through a wall separating them from women students in St Mary's. Needing moral courage to project an air of dignified outrage, Miss Lorimer 'put on her hat' to confront the young men.

Miss Lorimer's hat was apparently decorated with a pendant ostrich feather. In 1951, the twenty-four-year-old Margaret Roberts, a serious-minded graduate of Somerville College Oxford, married wealthy, divorced businessman Denis Thatcher, in London. She wore a full-length midnight blue velvet gown with a sweetheart neckline and matching muff and cap. The cap was garnished with a pendant ostrich feather. It was a highly romantic ensemble, like something out of a Gainsborough melodrama. Indeed, the outfit was allegedly inspired by the eighteenth-century Gainsborough painting of Georgiana, Duchess of Devonshire.

Margaret Thatcher loved clothes and put a great deal of thought into what she would wear. Early in her political career she sought to appeal to voters by dressing as a housewife and was photographed washing dishes at a kitchen sink. Between 1979 and 1990, as first woman prime minister of the United Kingdom, she crafted a carefully calibrated style of dressing to express authority, sensitivity to context and femininity. Her style became legendary and is regularly invoked as the quintessential example of power dressing in the 1980s. Several – though not all – of the 'rules' Molloy had articulated in 1977 were followed. The tailored skirt suit, often in blue, sometimes grey, was a staple of Thatcher's wardrobe. These outfits were often purchased from upmarket British clothing firm Aquascutum. The tailoring tended to be softened by a silky blouse, often with a 'pussy bow', and/or rows of pearls.

These touches signified femininity, and although Thatcher was relentlessly caricatured by the satirical TV puppet show *Spitting Image* as a cross-dresser, smoking fat cigars and addressed by her cabinet as 'Sir', she was rarely without some kind of feminine touch in her dress, be it the blouses, the bows or the brooches.

There was also the handbag. Thatcher's handbags were legendary. These were classy, boxy and traditional, from Asprey, Ferragamo or Launer. Molloy considered handbags (rather than attaché cases) the wrong choice for women seeking to establish authority. But Thatcher is credited with having inspired a new verbal usage: the handbag became weaponised, and the verb 'to handbag' came to mean a woman attacking someone, or some idea, with ruthlessness and force.

All in all, Thatcher *performed* femininity through her dress, and her performance generally showed an eye for political advantage. Aware of this, she could be playful, as in the extraordinary address she gave to Finchley Conservatives in 1976. 'I stand before you tonight, in my Red Star chiffon evening gown,' she announced on that occasion, 'my face softly made up and my fair hair gently waved, the "Iron Lady" of the Western world.' She went on to proclaim a cast-iron commitment to freedom and choice, and the audience loved it.

The term 'power dressing' passed into common usage in the 1980s. Women were benefitting from better education and a widening of opportunities for employment; they were delaying marriage and having children later in life, often choosing or needing to combine paid work and motherhood. The workplace could prove difficult territory for women, especially mothers, and a good deal of anxiety might be generated by efforts to juggle tasks and to secure promotion. What did ambitious women wear? If we scan the pages of fashion magazines such as *Vogue* or *Cosmopolitan*, there is a definite shift in the 1980s, a shift towards more assertive clothes. The term 'Glamazons' was often used from around this time. Power dressing frequently

CHAPTER SEVEN

Tailoring and shoulder pads: women looking businesslike, 1980s

came close to a kind of corporate drag during the 1980s, with mannish suits in pinstripe or hound's tooth fabrics, boasting massive shoulder pads. Women models were posed wearing collars and ties, with cropped hair, like surrogate males. An alternative was a kind of glitzy femininity with brocaded fabrics, rhinestones, sequins and sparkle and masses of gold jewellery. The shoulder pads were the same, but in the glitzy version of power dressing, women tended to have deep décolleté necklines and what became known as Big Hair. They often wore shoes with high, 'killer heels'. Like the heroines of popular TV shows *Dallas* and *Dynasty*, these women took up space.

Former editor of British *Vogue,* Alexandra Shulman, recalled an American aunt who was a successful businesswoman: this aunt had always worn suits. She had bought her niece her first suit, 'a pale grey Cerruti number with a fine pale blue stripe'. Its long jacket and slightly padded shoulders paired with a straight skirt gave it a slightly masculine look, Shulman remembered. It had proved serviceable: she had worn it to office events and job interviews throughout her twenties. 'When I wore it,' she mused, 'I felt exactly the way you were meant to feel in business suits – confident, smart, empowered.' This was in the early 1980s. In 1992 Shulman was appointed editor of British *Vogue*. As was the case with most of her young female colleagues in journalism and the media, she looked upon suits for women as an accepted part of office life. The idea was that power dressing would help them climb the professional ladder, she reflected, and yet 'fashion was ahead of the game'. In real life, promotions came slowly and there were few women in senior positions to act as role models. Shulman tells us that she bought a suit when she first became editor of *Vogue*. This suit was hardly conventional, since it was in slightly stretchy black fabric 'with a curved silver zip, like a scimitar, that ran across my breast'. But she had only bought three more suits in her twenty-five-year tenure as editor, she confessed: she had tired of their uniform-like quality.

A number of factors combined to undermine power dressing in the office. There was something of a backlash against the successful career woman who was accused of trying 'to have it all', and who went in for conspicuous consumption alongside career success. Films such as *The Devil Wears Prada* (2006) and *I Don't Know How She Does It* (2011, based on Allison Pearson's 2002 novel of the same title) suggested that women might be trying too hard to attain too many different goals. Women in senior and executive positions could be all too aware of conflicts between parenting and the workplace, between trying to project an image of themselves as Glamazons whilst surreptitiously wiping baby sick off the shoulder pads of their designer suits. And in the early twenty-first century, conventions about office wear softened a little in the context of a massive rise in the popularity of health regimes and the wearing of sportswear.

There was still plenty of evidence of conflicting expectations and persistent double standards. In 2016, Nicola Thorp, a young receptionist working for Portico, a third-party supplier of front-of-house and reception services for PricewaterhouseCoopers, was sent home for refusing to wear shoes with a 2–4-inch heel to work. She launched a petition against such regulations which eventually gained some 150,000 signatures. It resulted in an inquiry and joint report, 'High Heels and Workplace Dress Codes', from the House of Commons Petitions Committee and the Women and Equalities Committee. The upshot was that the government agreed to provide guidance to employers on the issues raised. It was pointed out that equalities legislation already provided for challenges to overt discrimination between men and women over dress codes. There was to be no change in the law.

Double standards remain in the sense that female politicians, particularly those in high office, are much more vulnerable to adverse comments in the press, but also from colleagues, about what they wear than are their male counterparts. It is very hard for them to get it right. Theresa May, the UK's second woman to serve as prime minister, generally played it safe with suits, or plain dress and jacket combinations. But slight variations from the code – her penchant for leopard-print kitten heels, or gobstopper necklaces, for instance, attracted attention, and at least on one occasion, when she was photographed wearing a pair of leather trousers in 2016, hostile comment. In an article in the *Guardian* headed 'Theresa May's leather trousers: you need a tough hide to wear them', Morwenna Ferrier considered the criticism of May's outfit – especially that of fellow female Conservative Nicky Morgan – who, commenting on the trousers' £995 price-tag, allegedly asserted that she personally hadn't ever spent that much on an outfit apart from her wedding dress. Ferrier wondered whether the jibes over the Amanda Wakeley leather trousers were because many people considered them 'expensive and fruity', pointing out that their cost paled into insignificance when one compared them with the price tag (around £3,500) of one of former prime minister David Cameron's custom-made suits.

The coronavirus pandemic had a dramatic impact on patterns of working life. Lockdowns meant offices and workplaces were often totally deserted as most people tried to work from home. Smart work clothes stayed in the wardrobe and sweatpants became standard daytime wear. There were plenty of jokes about how working through Zoom meetings or Microsoft Teams, you only had to think about what to wear *above* the waistline: no-one could see what you were wearing below. With a slow drift back to office life, there have been big shifts in work patterns and expectations about behaviour; it is probably still too early to appreciate which changes will prove permanent.

Towards the end of 2021, Helena Morrissey (Baroness Morrissey) published a book entitled *Style and Substance: A Career Guide for Women who Want to Win at Work*. It was described in the *Daily Mail* as 'a fiercely feminist guide to power dressing'. Baroness Morrissey, a financier and campaigner, has had an extraordinarily impressive career in corporate finance, combining this with being the mother of nine children. Part of her success in the City, she alleges, has been down to a deliberate focus on dress and appearance. Early in her career she had tended to go for a quiet professional look, but came to believe that the pale, feminised imitation of a male businessman was a mistake. One had to work at being oneself, to develop a 'personal brand' and to do this with confidence and style. Only then was there a chance of altering other people's perceptions of competence and potential. One should try to feel empowered, not encumbered, by one's femininity.

Can clothing empower? Dressing in certain ways can certainly make people feel more confident. It can bolster, help to dodge or challenge perceptions and prejudices. But it is hard to believe that dress alone can play a major part in upsetting power balance or changing systems. Clothes, style and fashion reflect social change or, more frequently, clothing choices are woven and refracted in complex ways through change. These choices are intricately tied up with shifts in power and authority, but it is unrealistic to invoke them as prime agents in the process.

EIGHT

Dress and Defiance

REPORTING ON PEOPLE'S REACTIONS to Dior's New Look in 1947, pioneering social research organisation Mass Observation (MO) noted that in spite of the 'apologia of the fashion houses', the immediate response was 'one of aggressive hostility', but that this had gone along with 'a defeatist feeling, among women, that they must succumb in the end'. A year later some respondents were again asked for their views. By then, it seemed, initial antipathy had declined, and most people had come to accept the new feminine silhouette. Older women were likely to see the long full skirt as dignified, Observers reported, with one middle-aged housewife commenting that such skirts hid 'the ravages to her legs of age'. Younger men could also show enthusiasm, one commenting that the New Look brought 'eagerly awaited glamour to an otherwise depressing world'. The older man 'who may have to buy the clothes', the MO report admitted, sometimes expressed more reservations. And then there was the vexed question of whether overly 'feminine' fashions – femininity 'writ large' – might undermine women's emancipation and sense of agency. Were women being tamed into compliance with fashion's edicts? Was the 'masculine, capable, efficient, strong-willed female' now to be 'out of fashion'?

Much of the Mass Observation material on dress and fashion

through the period 1939–54 reflects a defensiveness, sometimes shading into a defiant repudiation of fashion as something irrelevant and silly, at least on the part of the Observed. Tom Harrisson, with Humphrey Jennings and Charles Madge, one of the founders of MO, found the subject fascinating. In a press release describing recent work on the subject in 1939, he marvelled at how fashions from Paris which caught on in the West End of London often reached the poorer industrial districts of big cities within a few days. He was fascinated by 'the bottom of the ladder, the forty million British who don't own a diamond' and how fashion got through to them. Mass Observers asked people where they thought the latest fashions came from: 23% thought Paris, 21% Hollywood. Another 9% thought royalty, 6% 'the Jews'. Only 3% thought fashion emanated from magazines. But a whacking great 36% 'didn't know or care'.

Several women seemed to be irritated by the questioning. There was a concern among the married women not to provoke their husbands' disapproval, either through spending too much on themselves or by trying to look too glamorous. A thirty-seven-year-old woman in the East End confessed to an Observer that she had wanted to dye her hair blonde but her husband wouldn't let her, asking what on earth she was thinking about, who did she think she was doing it for, a woman with three children? Younger women were more interested in clothes and cosmetics, but needed to be careful with money: much of their interest went into wistful window shopping or purchasing cheap stuff from Woolworths. They sometimes got riled by MO questioning. A twenty-seven-year-old woman, asked whether she followed fashion, retorted, 'Do I bloody hell? I haven't any money, idiot.'

MO concluded from its wartime surveys that only about one in thirty women confessed to taking any interest in fashion. Most liked a warm coat when the old one got too shabby, and a new hat to liven things up, but, particularly after marriage, the majority of women didn't see fashion as having much relevance in their lives. Observers noticed that younger women in the East End of London were often smartly dressed, stylish and even glamorous: after the age of about forty-five they seemed often to give up, happy to be seen in print overalls and bedroom slippers, even in the street. Major social changes after the war included the growing importance of teenage spending, particularly during the late 1950s and 1960s; the increasing availability of inexpensive, manufactured clothing, and the expanding circulation of women's magazines. With rising standards of living, did fashion assume a more important role in more women's lives? It is interesting to compare the evidence from Mass Observation's Spring Directive in 1988, which set out to investigate attitudes to clothing, with the earlier material.

The majority of Mass Observers replying to the 1988 Directive showed themselves defiantly uninterested in fashion, although much invested in what they wore. Most were careful about spending and seriously interested in comfort. There was a general antipathy to 'labels', and to people who dressed to create an impression, or who wore 'unsuitable' clothing. This applied to both men and women. Most people confessed to owning a large amount of clothing. One of the suggestions made in the guiding notes issued to respondents was that they should conduct an inventory of their wardrobes, listing all the items of clothing that they possessed. Many demurred, seeing this as too onerous a task, although a surprising number made a valiant effort to comply. Most people admitted to keeping clothes that they no longer wore for various reasons, such as sentimental associations, or a hope that they would lose weight which they had put on since the items were last worn. Several women confessed that they still cherished clothes that were several decades old. One woman wrote of a jersey dress made by her niece some twenty-two years ago: her mother had crocheted two sets of collars and cuffs for it in different colours and she loved it: it washed and pressed 'like a dream'.

It was common for respondents to emphasise thrift and economy. They boasted of sales bargains, of clothes that had been acquired second-hand, of using a daughter's cast-offs, and of repurposing things. One lady proudly announced that her old clothes went to 'the Third World' or were sewn into cushions for her cat to sleep on. Older women liked clothes that were roomy and comfortable and many emphasised a desire to fit in, to look respectable and not to draw attention to themselves. There were one or two nostalgic comments lamenting the demise of *Vogue*'s Mrs Exeter. A few women noted that their personal dress style had been forged many years ago and hadn't changed since. Respondents could be quite judgemental about other people's clothes, particularly about women who could be accused of dressing inappropriately for their age, and of looking like 'mutton dressed as lamb'.

In part this judgementalism was elicited in response to one of the prompts offered by the Directive, which asked people to comment on what they considered 'flash' in dressing. There were some interesting replies. 'Flash' is 'too bright, too tight, too exaggerated, too glittery, too short', suggested one Observer. Flash 'in a woman is long red fingernails and wreeking [sic] of Estée Lauder's Youth Dew', wrote another. Flash brought to mind 'tight jeans, high heels, gold ankle chains, a jumper with feathers or glitter of some sort and a fur coat', offered another respondent. The popularity of soap operas *Dallas* and *Dynasty* on British TV in the late 1980s contributed to the fashion for glitz and glitter at that time, so that these respondents' comments indicate some defiance of contemporary trends. There was a widespread disapproval for what was perceived as 'vulgar'. 'I think I would describe women as common, rather than flash,' wrote one respondent, revealing attitudes which had probably been shaped in childhood.

There were some replies which stood out as bucking the general trend towards discreet worthiness. A woman who admitted going for comfort, durability and low cost confessed that she kept two 'dramatic items' in her wardrobe: a green and red Chinese dragon dress, and what she thought of as her 'daring dress', because it had such a low neckline. But taking care not to stand out, she didn't wear these garments. She was more likely to go for a tracksuit with an old anorak. Another female respondent was less restrained in her fantasy. Clothes had always been important to her, and she fondly reminisced about the dance dresses of the 1950s, the frilly petticoats and full taffeta skirts. Invited to a party at her husband's golf club one Christmas Eve, she had chosen to wear fuchsia Courtelle with a plunging neckline, tight waist and full, ruffled skirt. She admitted to having been quite gratified by the disapproval this dress seems to have provoked amongst the older women present, who she dismissed as '*grandes dames*' wearing 'brown crepe with artificial flowers'. She had been delighted when one 'dear old gentleman' had 'tottered over' to her to declare 'My dear, you look delicious – just like a page out of *Esquire*!'

In his book *Fashion, Culture and Identity* (1992), sociologist Fred Davis drew a distinction between people who were indifferent to fashion and those who took a stand in opposition to it. Those who were *anti-fashion*, he saw as actively in dialogue with fashion trends. Anti-fashion could take many forms, he suggested: it might stem from utilitarian outrage, from feminist protest, from countercultural beliefs, for example. He suggested that since the 1960s, the speeding up of fashion cycles and the growth of fashion pluralism had weakened the dialectical relationship between fashion and anti-fashion.

We can often see resonance and parallels between 'high' fashion and subcultural trends which reinforce the idea of a dialogue. Film director Ken Russell took a wonderful series of photographs of Teddy Girls in London in the 1950s. Dressed

CHAPTER EIGHT

Ken Russell photograph of Teddy girls, 1950s

stylishly, and with meticulous attention to detail, they pose against graffitied, tumbledown walls and bomb-damaged homes and workplaces. The girls were from ordinary working-class homes, with limited resources to spend on clothes. Their outfits have been described as a fusion of Edwardian elegance with beatnik rebellion: the feminine equivalent of the Teddy Boy style. But we can also see the borrowings from *haute couture* in the 1950s in these photographs – the slim, sharp-pointed umbrellas, gloves and clutch bags, shawl collars, ballet shoes and glittering statement jewellery. There are also similarities of pose and demeanour with the fashion photography of the day. The girls stare proudly and directly into the camera, there is a defiance in their body language which recalls that of fifties models such as Dovima, Lisa Fonssagrives, Suzy Parker or Dorian Leigh.

From mid-century on, trends in fashion appear to have moved in at least two directions, with 'high' fashion percolating down through society from Paris and the fashion centres of Europe and America, but also with popular street style and subcultural trends increasingly likely to influence designers at the centre of the industry. The Youthquake of the 1960s and 1970s had a huge effect on the fashion and clothing industries, bringing many young designers (Mary Quant, Barbara Hulanicki, Ossie Clark, Celia Birtwell, Alice Pollock) into prominence in Britain. Miniskirts, 'unisex' gender-bending clothes and the kind of vintage nostalgia which inspired Quorum and Biba might start as trends independent of the big fashion houses but would eventually influence their collections. Countercultural styles such as punk and grunge might gain impetus from a powerful sense of transgression and defiance, but were always in danger of losing edge, as elements of the style entered the mainstream.

The history of punk is instructive. In the UK, punk rock rose to prominence in the mid-1970s with the Sex Pistols, Malcolm McLaren and Vivienne Westwood. Associated with both rock music and fashion, punk proliferated, with different forms and strands. The styling of pop legend Madonna's early performances owed much to punk, particularly the clothes: her semi-transparent mesh tops, black lace gloves and messy, backcombed hair. Punk can also be seen as feeding into the 'kinderwhore' style of subversive femininity associated with Riot Grrrls in the US, and with female grunge bands such as Kat Bjelland and Babes in Toyland or Courtney Love and Hole.

Punk's keynote was defiance. Adopted by women, it offered an unambiguous challenge to norms of conventional femininity: discretion, the neat and the demure. The lyrics of punk rock

CHAPTER EIGHT

Girl punk, Camden, 1980s

girl bands – such as the Slits' *Typical Girls* – railed against the limited choices seen as offered to young women. And there was the unstoppable eloquence of the clothes. Viv Albertine recalled how she used to walk around in little girls' party dresses, torn, slashed and ragged. Her bleached-blonde hair was unkempt, her eyes smudged with black eyeliner. She completed the look with fishnet tights and shocking pink boots from the shop called simply 'Sex'. The look asked for, and often got her into, trouble. The group was sometimes thrown out of hotels. Viv herself was aware that she had crossed the line from 'sexy wild girl just fallen out of bed' to something 'unpredictable, dangerous, unstable': 'Pippi Longstocking meets Barbarella meets juvenile delinquent'. She added that men looked at her and got confused. They weren't sure whether they wanted 'to fuck me or kill me', concluding, 'This sartorial ensemble really messes with their heads. Good.'

Many designers were influenced by the energy of punk. In Britain, Zandra Rhodes' Conceptual Chic collection in 1977 featured slashed and torn designs, sometimes fastened together with gold safety pins. In 1994, actress Liz Hurley created a media sensation when she was photographed at the premier of her then boyfriend Hugh Grant's film, *Four Weddings and a Funeral*, wearing a black dress by Versace, hugely revealing, and basically held together by a row of outsize gold safety pins. Versace's 1997 collection was directly influenced by punk culture. Hedi Slimane's designs for Yves St Laurent in 2015–16 took inspiration from punk and grunge and featured models looking like bedraggled prom queens crowned with rhinestone tiaras.

Did all this neutralise the subversive energy of punk? In their book, *Fashioning the Feminine* (2002), design historians Cheryl Buckley and Hilary Fawcett saw punk in the late 1970s as providing some young women with 'a truly radical visual identity: an uncompromising rejection of norms of femininity' which was charged with the momentum of second-wave feminism. But they see this as having been a missed opportunity for a full engagement with the themes of gender and identity. Even so, punk as a sensibility, sometimes morphing into new forms, has never completely gone away. It speaks to and for groups of young women even in the 2020s about defiance, and a challenging form of femininity.

NINE

Mail Order, Mirrors and Murmurations

DURING THE CORONAVIRUS PANDEMIC in the UK, more and more people had to abandon any idea of going to the shops and began, instead, to order goods online. In March 2020, around 40% of UK shoppers reported shopping more online. A year later this percentage had increased to about 75%. For many years I had travelled from Brighton to buy clothes in London. Agnès B. and Zadig&Voltaire were my favourite stores. But from March 2019 up to the spring of 2022 I joined the general trend, scrutinising the latest offerings from both brands online, agonising over what I might look like in items that caught my eye, and waiting in excitedly (and often with frustration) for parcels to arrive.

We sometimes think of internet shopping as a recent trend, but mail ordering clothes is a practice that goes back to the nineteenth century. In Newtown, on the Welsh border, a former draper's apprentice with an entrepreneurial bent, Pryce Jones, began selling goods made from Welsh flannel, which he posted to all parts of the country and soon, abroad. His printed catalogue of 1861 was attractive and divided into sections, something like a department store. His list of goods diversified and orders came from prestigious sources, including Queen Victoria, Florence Nightingale, foreign royalty and the Russian army. In 1879, the year he was knighted, Pryce Jones built a huge warehouse near the railway line, boasting of having some 100,000 customers by 1880. The warehouse was expanded in 1895 and again in 1901: the factory had acquired its own post office that year.

Several mail-order firms were founded in the UK in the early twentieth century: famous names include the Bradford-based Empire Stores, Littlewoods, Great Universal Stores, Grattan Warehouses, Kays of Worcester and Freemans. Most flourished particularly after the Second World War, producing elaborate seasonal catalogues, listing clothing and often all manner of household and domestic goods, and significantly expanding their share of the retail market. Whilst tempting to suggest parallels between the British and American experience, and in particular with the huge importance of the Sears Roebuck enterprise in the US, recent research has drawn attention to the ways in which the British development of mail order was distinctive. The market for mail-order clothing in Britain tended to come from lower-income households, which were as likely to be in urban and suburban areas as in the remoter countryside. British firms expanded on the base of easy instalment credit and a network of commercial agents, usually women, who had close community and family ties and who were trusted by both buyer and seller as go-betweens. One recent history has suggested that in the 1960s there were as many as 2.5 million active agents working for mail-order firms. Working-class women tended to associate buying goods from a catalogue with 'Auntie Katheen' or 'Joan from down the street', and this experience of shopping could be far less daunting than a trip to a posh department store. Easy credit, with payment through small instalments, suited wives without their own bank accounts and with limited resources.

It has been estimated that in the 1960s around half of all households saw a mail-order clothing catalogue every year. These catalogues were often huge, especially those advertising household goods alongside clothing for all the family. And they could be extremely attractive. Early twentieth-century clothing catalogues now look like works of art, especially those issued by department stores (Bradleys, Dickens & Jones and Peter Robinson, for instance) around the First World War. They can be full of delicate line drawings showing elaborate, lace-encrusted blouses, tea gowns, corsetry and underwear. They are avidly collected by those with interests in vintage costume. But the mail-order catalogues from the postwar years are also impressive, and a wonderful source of information for dress historians. They make it possible, for instance, for us to get a sense of how quickly and to what extent 'high' fashion reached 'ordinary' women, especially those living at a distance from London and the larger provincial shopping centres.

Glancing through the pages of Marshall Ward, Littlewoods and Empire Stores catalogues from the 1950s, we can see that they offered clothes that were up-to-the-minute in fashion terms alongside more serviceable and standard items. In 1954, Marshall Ford advertised a 'fabulously full' circle skirt in 'art silk taffeta' with large, richly embroidered motifs around the hemline. This cost 42s 6d, and could be teamed with a Brigitte Bardot-style off-the-shoulder blouse edged with a silk fringe at 22s 6d. A straight-backed 'swagger coat' in 'soft-toned shadow check wool material' could be had for as little as £11 10s. Littlewoods' 1956 catalogue featured summer dresses with very full skirts in 'glamourised cotton'; one example trimmed in white ricrac braid was described as made-up in 'peacock green iced fabric, a luscious rustly cotton' and sold for 55s. The dresses hint at Dior's New Look with their tightly cinched-in waists, and they were cheaper than Horrockses. The Empire Stores catalogue offerings for 1957–58 included some particularly fashionable items. Their circle skirt was in a 'Venetian Red' felt, with diamond-shaped pockets, it was teamed with another Bardot-style off-the-shoulder top, this time a black sweater; on the opposite page a model posed on a Vespa scooter sporting a white duffel coat over tapered slacks and ballet pumps.

Mail-order clothing companies had previously developed many of the techniques common in twenty-first century internet shopping, from attractive and detailed catalogues (websites) to sizing charts, and easy returns. Making it easy for customers to return garments which failed to fit, or which didn't meet expectations, has always been important. Many of today's companies have gone one step further, encouraging customers to order a clutch of items in the expectation that most of these will be tried on, but sent back. Digital technology makes more innovation possible. The three-dimensional modelling of customers' bodies and simulation of individuals trying on different garments is technically possible. Walmart has introduced 'virtual fitting rooms' where customers can 'try out' different clothes to see how they would look: this technology is likely to be improved and refined over the next few years.

Screens can act as mirrors. You can key in your personal details – body measurements, skin and hair colour, age and fashion preferences – and an algorithm will provide suggestions for a 'look'. Screens facilitate the editing of appearance in many ways. There are innumerable videos giving instructions in, and demonstrations of, the wearing of clothes, hairstyles and techniques of make-up. Many women post regular photographs of themselves on Instagram or Facebook. Is this obsession with 'selfies' a form of narcissism, or a seeking of validation and approval, an expression of vulnerability? It is most likely a combination of these things.

Both young and older women seek appreciation and approval. Baroness Helena Morrissey's recent book *Style and Substance* was mentioned earlier in these pages. From 2019, Morrissey began regularly posting photographs of herself in whatever she was wearing on that day on Instagram. She tells us that she started this 'career dressing' account on Instagram because so many women were asking her what they should wear to work. By most people's standards, Morrissey's career in the finance industry has been stellar. She has combined this with motherhood and social and political activism. And yet she admits to personal insecurities about ageing and appearance. When she first started posting images of herself, she opted for a Zara dress, admitting that she was nervous about wearing anything too expensive. Later she 'upped her style game', confidently posing in expensive designer dresses against a background of gold curtains and usually accompanied by her pet dog, Buddy. Morrissey tells us that she delights in the 'conversations' and the 'camaraderie' that follow through other women's comments on her looks, noting that it is 'the spectacular' gowns which attract the most 'likes', alongside her own comments, particularly when these display a certain amount of vulnerability.

Helena Morrissey points out that her energetic posting of selfies on Instagram gained impetus from lockdown during the Covid pandemic. Getting dressed – or, more particularly, getting dressed up – provided a psychological boost to many women who slouched around in tracksuits, lonely and a bit bored through long days of being confined to the home. The internet provided platforms and a stage where individuals could confess and share experiences directly, as well as mirrors in which they could survey and edit their appearance, reacting to the comments and appraisal of others. Sometimes the excessive posting of selfies seems to go too far. One is reminded of the Wicked Queen in Snow White: 'Mirror, mirror, on the wall/Who is the fairest of them all?' There can definitely be a competitive, perfectionist element in all this which can be damaging to appearance-obsessed young women. But learning about style and developing preferences is also a form of self-education.

The ways in which the internet has influenced fashion and

how we dress are many and varied. We might consider, for instance, the influence of catwalk shows online, the expansion of a finely nuanced market for vintage clothing, the emergence of 'social media influencers', the proliferation of choice and the development of niche communities. A search for fashion subcultures on the internet yields a rich and sometimes bewildering variety. There are the familiar and resilient goth/punk/grunge trends. 'Dark Academia' brings together a Harry Potter-ish aesthetic with preppiness, Oxbridge and Ivy League. 'Regency core' references the popular TV series, *Bridgerton*, as much as Jane Austen or Beau Brummel. 'Cottage core' harks back to Laura Ashley and roses-round-the door, with strong touches of homespun, pretty china and Cath Kidston. 'Clown core' is bobbles, neck-frills and brightness, with the inevitable undercurrent of sadness and melancholy. And then there are 'e-girls and e-boys' mainly exhibiting on TikTok. How does fashion move or diffuse? It is no longer adequate to think of trends as either starting at the top and seeping down through society, nor of street fashion percolating up into *couture*. The fashion scene, on the internet and as represented in social media generally, shows trends that swirl and divide, swell, swoop and are suddenly gone like a murmuration of starlings or shoal of brightly coloured fish.

TEN

Glamour and Feminism

AS I GREW UP IN THE 1950S I vaguely realised that glamour was dangerous territory. At home, women who looked glamorous might be described as 'no better than they should be', or 'all fur coat and no knickers'. It had something to do with peroxided blonde hair, and red lipstick or nail varnish. There were also fur coats, of course, and those conical, circle-stitched 1950s bras, shaping breasts into twin peaks beneath tight black sweaters. Mum, in her beige pleated crimplene, went a bit pursed-lipped and clearly disapproved. And so did the teachers at school, who lived in an entirely different world. Did glamour have something to do with sexual predatoriness? I think I half-suspected something along those lines. It was clearly dodgy because it had something to do with sex.

The word 'glamour' originally conveyed the idea of illusion, or enchantment. Sir Walter Scott is credited with the use of the term in the nineteenth century, associating glamour with witchcraft and magic. The word came into its own with the development of Hollywood cinema and the popularity of 'screen goddesses' in the 1930s. Black-and-white cinema intensified the effects of light; shimmer and sparkle, the play of light on rich fabrics, dark satins and white-blonde hair. Screen goddesses and personalities such as Marlene Dietrich, Mae West, Greta Garbo and Jean Harlow were the epitome of glamour, enacting a go-getting form of femininity, sophisticated and sexually aware.

In America, the Motion Picture Production (Hays) Code was to clamp down on permissiveness and the portrayal of sexually liberated women after 1934 and up until the late 1950s. In Britain, too, there was always a vein of popular unease about glamour. It might be seen as too American, too slick. Inherent in the idea of illusion was a suggestion of falsity. English girls, with their supposed lack of sophistication, their homeliness and modesty, were often fêted as more authentic, natural and unspoiled than their American counterparts. And in the upper-class society of the Shires, glamour could look vulgar.

A tendency to look on glamour as trying too hard, or as slightly brash, became apparent after the war in a Britain full of deference for royalty and traditional values. The marriage of Princess Elizabeth to Philip Mountbatten and the Coronation of the young Queen in 1953 were events which celebrated class, hierarchy and a profoundly conservative form of gender relations. This was a society where little girls dreamed of becoming princesses. The term 'mannequin' was much more acceptable than 'glamour model', which might imply hand-written, fly-blown advertisements in corner-shop windows. Model schools, such as the famous establishment of Lucie Clayton, taught elocution, deportment, charm and manners. Glamour became associated with the antics of publicity-seeking celebrities such as Diana Dors, Jayne Mansfield and 'Sabrina' (Norma Ann Sykes), regularly flaunting their bosoms and their sexual charms in the popular press. 'Blonde Bombshell' Diana Dors, for instance, made headlines at the Venice Film Festival in 1955 when she took a ride in a gondola down the Grand Canal wearing nothing but an (allegedly) mink bikini.

Glamour is a slithery concept, not least because both the use of the word and its meaning have shifted through time. When used to denote a particular style, the word harks back to the 1930s, a kind of 'glamour of Hollywood' gold standard: this is usually what fashion writers mean when they talk about 'old-fashioned glamour'. As a style, further, the word connotes sophistication and a degree of theatricality. Glamour is performative. It is more appropriate to describe a slinky crepe or satin Biba dress as glamorous than a Laura Ashley flowered smock; Laura Ashley dresses aimed to suggest an innocent girlish naturalness rather than sophistication. Many fashion trends of the 1980s epitomised glamour: glitz, lamé and leopardskin, blood-red lips and nails all accord with theatricality, confidence and a certain brashness or even vulgarity. When Mass Observers were asked about clothing in the 1980s, they were questioned as to what they understood by 'flash' dressing. Their answers show them united in thinking that this meant glitz and brashness, hallmarks of the then popular TV shows *Dallas* and *Dynasty*. But by the end of the century the terms glamour and glamorous were used so widely in fashion journalism and women's magazines as to connote almost anything considered to have style.

The late 1960s and early 1970s saw the rise of the women's liberation movement in Britain, often referred to as 'second-wave feminism'. During this time glamour became something of a dirty word, associated with the sexual objectification of women. Beauty pageants and beauty contests were popular events all over the country, but for many feminists they were a degrading form of 'cattle market'. The 1970 Miss World Competition at the Albert Hall was famously disrupted by feminists incensed by the patronising, misogynistic remarks of the compère, the hapless Bob Hope, who was flour-bombed and pelted with rotten fruit. 'We're not beautiful, we're not ugly, we're angry,' announced a feminist leaflet at the time.

The politics of beauty competitions weren't simple, though. The 1970 contest has been heralded as the first time a black woman (Jennifer Hosten, Miss Grenada) won the Miss World title. Others claim that Carole Joan Crawford (Miss Jamaica) was the first non-white woman to win the title, in 1963. Beauty contests were often popular amongst black activists who wanted to challenge the idea that beauty was inextricable from whiteness. In Britain, the radical politician Claudia Jones (founder of the *West Indian Gazette* and 'Mother of the Notting Hill Carnival') promoted black women's beauty contests as a celebration of cultural identity, alongside her interest in encouraging women to set up hairdressing salons for African-Caribbean women in London.

I didn't come across feminist ideas in any real sense whilst at school, or even at university. There was little or no mention of women in the undergraduate history syllabus that I followed at Reading in the late 1960s. It was only many years later, studying the history of women in universities, that I discovered that a number of interesting women with feminist ideas had taught there at one time or another. In 1908, literary scholar Edith Morley had been the first woman to be appointed to a university chair in Britain, although her appointment had been controversial, and Reading had not treated her kindly: it promoted her with reluctance and had given her a hard time. Morley had died in 1964. Other women teachers had included the economist Mabel Buer (1881–1942); sociologist Viola Klein (1908–1973), remembered not least for her work on the social construction of femininity; another sociologist, Margaret Scotford Archer (then Scotford-Morton) and for a while, the celebrated feminist Juliet Mitchell. The last three women had been teaching whilst I was a student there, but Margaret Archer was the only one I came into contact with. She had given lectures to first-year students. They were very theoretical, and I'm afraid that what I remember most vividly, apart from her confident and forceful delivery, was that she was an incredibly stylish dresser. A caramel leather blouson jacket comes to mind, even after all these years.

'Second-wave' feminism didn't really hit me until I found myself teaching in higher education, and at that point, it hit me with the force of revelation. It gave shape to many of the areas of friction and resentment that I had felt, growing up. I read avidly, excited by the new developments in feminist and women's history, discovering a new passion for research into the past. It is hard to remember how I felt about academic work before becoming a feminist: I was ever interested in ideas, but my connection with them was always somewhat distanced. Now, I really cared. And it all added up.

I remember thinking a lot about women's relationship to scholarship and the curriculum. With feminist colleagues, I started introducing new courses on women's history at the University of Sussex, where I had become a lecturer. One year I discovered the collection of letters about maternity and experiences of motherhood which were collected by the Women's Co-operative Guild in 1915. It was then out of print, but I managed to get a copy. I thought my mother might be interested, and gave it to her. She couldn't put it down. What was moving was her complete disbelief and incomprehension that something of such interest to her could be 'taught' at a university. Mum had left school at fifteen. She never had understood my interest in books. But suddenly she did. It was a lesson in how different experiences of education might be, when the curriculum has relevance to the learner.

I became very involved in feminist history in the 1970s. Having always had a consuming interest in clothes, perfume and cosmetics, I was sometimes disconcerted by the way other feminists dressed. From time to time I found myself troubled about how I must look through the eyes of those who I suspected were better feminists than me. Was it pathetic to dress in a way which might be construed as trying to attract men? Did I look tarty and insincere? Many colleagues appeared happy to go about in jeans or even dungarees, wearing no make-up. I rarely went out without ringing my eyes in kohl, usually wore lipstick and *always* perfume. I spent a lot of time – too much time, I admitted, ruefully – obsessing about what I wore. Earlier in these pages I recounted one episode where I guiltily tried to rub mascara and eye-black off with a tissue in the basement loo of A Woman's Place on the Victoria Embankment. I didn't want to look like a dollybird.

For a while, I think feminism did influence the way I dressed, although it isn't easy to separate out practical considerations. With two children, a full-time job and a commuting marriage (my husband and I lived apart much of the time, having university jobs in Brighton and Cambridge, a marriage which friends sometimes dubbed 'telegamy'), I was always insanely busy and hadn't time for too much frippery. I remember going for outfits that felt 'workmanlike'. There were the needlecord boiler suits in the late seventies, worn tightly belted. They felt good, although it was a palaver when one needed to pee.

Feminism's critique of the politics of appearance hotted up in the 1980s and 1990s. There was a great deal of concern over body shape, and young women's obsession with diet and exercise. Susie Orbach published her influential book *Fat is a Feminist Issue* in 1979. Against a background of fashionable excess in the 1980s, American feminist Susan Faludi argued that the fashion and cosmetics industries of that decade, with their promotion of models of glamourised femininity, were part of a backlash against the feminism of the 1970s. Naomi Wolf's *The Beauty Myth* (1990) was widely read, particularly by younger women in North America and Britain. Wolf saw glamourised images of femininity 'the beauty myth' – as central to women's oppression. She was a bit evasive about the pleasures of self-adornment. Whilst conceding that these existed, and that women might enjoy glamour and fantasy, she maintained that the real problem was that contemporary social pressures made for an insidious lack of choice and compulsion.

But an uncompromising attack on what feminist philosopher Sandra Lee Bartky called 'the fashion-beauty complex', and which she saw as paralleling 'the military industrial complex' in buttressing capitalist patriarchy, was never going to have widespread appeal. And by the end of the century, younger women were sometimes uneasy and confused about just what feminism stood for. Were feminists hostile to fashion? Did they reject cosmetics? Were they anti-men? Bartky conceded that feminists were widely regarded as 'enemies of the stiletto heel and the beauty parlour – in a word, as enemies of glamour', and that this had undermined its appeal to many women.

It was around this time that I found myself thinking about glamour, the history of the word, and what it had meant to women in the past. I had always taken notes when reading women's autobiographies, intrigued by how their memories so often revolved around what they had worn, how much they had dreamed about clothes and how they had cherished hopes of particular outfits having the potential to transform their lives. Jane Walsh, for instance, who had grown up in a poor Catholic family in Lancashire in the 1920s, reflected in the 1950s upon the fact that like many women, she found herself dating things by remembering what she had worn at the time. As a young woman, she had made herself a blue coat-frock in some cheap, coarse serge. She had 'spent hours and hours embroidering it with tiny beads', beaded trimmings being the height of fashion just then. She remembered how her coat had brought many admiring glances from male friends, and how she had been able to swagger a little, wearing it. Then there was Joan Wyndham, as a young woman in Chelsea on the eve of the Second World War, remembering the pleasures of Max Factor's pancake foundation, and delighting in the new cyclamen-coloured lipstick she had found in Woolworths. Or Nerina Shute, a controversial journalist and film critic in London between the wars: Shute wrote a racy memoir detailing her life and loves (she was bisexual), which she entitled *We Mixed Our Drinks* (1945). She describes how peroxiding her hair, and a combination of careful make-up (Max Factor, again) and sharp tailoring allowed her to transform herself into 'a glamour girl'. Dressed to the nines, she tucked a white poodle under her arm and sashayed down Bond Street, enjoying the effect she created, but later decided to abandon such artifice in favour of a more natural look.

When I decided to write a book on the history of glamour, and its relation to feminism, some colleagues were amused. I had built an academic career around work on the history of women's education and it might have looked like an abrupt change. 'So it's out of the bluestockings and into the fishnets, is it?' quipped the late literary scholar, Laura Marcus. But there was continuity in this. I was increasingly interested in women's changing aspirations, their dreams and desires, and how one might research these things. Appearance, like education, I reflected, offered fantasies of becoming. I had always enjoyed vintage clothes fairs, and the jumbles of discarded jewellery, old scent bottles, powder compacts and the like which could be found in car boot sales: what might be called 'the paraphernalia of femininity'. These interests chimed, too, with historians' growing general interest in material culture. My book, *Glamour, History, Feminism* was published by Zed Books in 2010, and the research which went into it was pure pleasure.

ELEVEN

Scent Trails

CLOTHES CAN BE MARKERS FOR MEMORIES, but this is even more true of scent and smell, which can trigger recall of emotions and experiences in the past in a powerfully direct way. In several of the photographs my parents took of me in early childhood I have my nose in a rose, and I remember vividly the heady pleasure of this, standing on tiptoe in our small suburban garden in order to reach the flowers.

I've always been passionately interested in perfumes. When I was very young my father, a pharmacist, worked for Timothy Whites & Taylors, a dispensing chemist and cosmetic store in Birmingham. Later, he acquired his own chemist shop in a suburban village in the Midlands. The shop was a source of wonder, with its ancient glass and ceramic jars, its dried roots and herbs and curious substances (water glass, slippery elm, liquorice root and lumps of copal resin). It was an old-established shop, and many potions and lotions were actually made in the dispensary. My earliest 'paid job', working for pocket money, involved helping to make a lurid pink hand-cream which had to be stirred over a stove in a huge saucepan in a shed round the back. As I remember, the ingredients included rosewater, glycerine and cochineal. Maybe beeswax or shea butter, too. The concoction had to be decanted into clean bottles and labelled. It was purchased immediately by old ladies in the vicinity, who swore by it. Dad didn't want to be bothered to make it anymore and tried to get the old ladies to buy commercially available brands instead, but they weren't having any of it, and it was a slow process. I remember his relief when he felt he could stop making the stuff.

The first scents that I remember were ones displayed prominently in the shop: Elizabeth Arden's Blue Grass and Mémoire Chérie. I was going through a pony phase at the time and the Blue Grass advertising material involved a romantic model horse in an extraordinary shade of blue, somewhere between turquoise and eau-de-nil, amply garlanded with flowers. I was smitten. One of Dad's assistants dressed the shop window in an old-fashioned way, nestling the horse in a riot of draped and tumbled satin with a vase of fresh foxgloves by his side. I remember the point-of-sale material much more vividly than the scents themselves, though, which have lodged in my mind as nice but not exciting, rather flowery and powdery.

My father often brought home samples of cosmetics, together with used and discarded testers for lipstick colours and perfumes. I remember particularly a set of Chanel perfumes, a coffret with scent bottles nestling in line. The scents were Cuir de Russie, Bois des Îles, N°5 and Gardénia. Gardénia was exotic-flowery and N°5 was famous and lovely but Cuir de Russie and Bois des Îles were astonishing and quite wonderful. I fell in love with both of these creations, the one buttery-leathery soft, the other hauntingly enticing and romantic. I know now that these were the work of perfume genius Ernest Beaux, responsible for Chanel N°5 and also for Bourjois' hugely successful popular fragrance of the 1930s and 1940s, Soir de Paris. For a long time in the 1970s and beyond I found Cuir de Russie and Bois des Îles impossible to get hold of. When Chanel reintroduced them in their *Les Exclusifs* range I was in heaven, and have rarely been without bottles of these two scents ever since.

CHAPTER ELEVEN

Advert for Elizabeth Arden's Blue Grass perfume, 1950s

My relationship with my father was close during childhood and early adolescence. We didn't talk a lot about perfume but were both interested; me as an incipient perfume junkie, Dad from a more commercial point of view. I spent quite a lot of my pocket money on scent. I bought bottles of Fenjal and the bath oil form of Estée Lauder's Youth Dew, and spent hours in hot baths, soaking away muscle cramp from horse-riding and the tensions of O- and A-Level examination marathons. I made the house steamy with strong scent. And stroppy hormones too, probably.

In late adolescence things got difficult with my father, who didn't take kindly to my 'plastering my face with make-up' and eyeing up unsuitable young men on motorbikes. The situation quite often blew up and we had explosive arguments, until the time I left home to go to university in the late sixties. Dad still bought me perfume for birthday and Christmas presents, by my own request: he always asked me what I wanted. He was enthusiastic about 1950s Rochas scents, I remember, especially Femme, which he assured me that the Queen had worn (I've no idea where this information came from). Femme came in a bottle shaped like womanly hips, the package adorned with black lace. It smelled of rich golden fruit. Definitely not my style. While at university I acquired a liking for Worth's Je Reviens, a favourite of some of my fellow students. It came in a fluted blue glass bottle and smelt a bit edgy, like hyacinths, silvery and intense. Dad bowed to my taste and bought me a large supply one Christmas.

I recently consulted perfume expert Luca Turin's writings about Je Reviens (Maurice Blanchet, 1932). Turin came up with some characteristically brilliant prose. The original scent gave the impression of 'an extraordinary opal green glow', he suggested, 'the sort that emanates from a numinous uncut gem in a Rider Haggard epic'. It was 'a strange, abstract, curiously artificial construction, part biker girl, part bluestocking'.

Wow. In retrospect, that is pretty much exactly what, at that time, I had aspired to be.

Thinking about Je Reviens, some half century after wearing it, made me curious, and a touch nostalgic, so I sought out a vintage bottle on the internet. It arrived looking authentic, in yellowing, faded packaging. But the scent had suffered and gone slightly petrol-sour. There was enough to remind me of what it had been, though. And I had to ask myself whether my own 'nose' has changed over the years. 'Wear it to attract someone of above average intelligence,' opines Turin. Hmm. There's still a bit of me that wants to appear part bluestocking, part biker girl. I bought a new leather jacket, not so long ago. But these days, if I wear leather, I'm likely to opt for a faint whiff of Le Labo Santal, or better still, Cuir de Russie. Writer Susan Irvine recollected the legendary *parfumeur* Edmond Roudnitska once describing a perfect scent as 'a beautiful flower snapped into a new leather handbag', noting that for her, this epitomised the charm of Ernest Beaux's Cuir de Russie, and I agree.

Fashions in scent change, and I followed them fairly closely during the 1970s and 1980s. With a full-time job, a husband who worked many miles away and two small children, my life was frenetically busy, but I was never too busy not to keep up my interest in perfume. It was both pleasure and solace, something akin to a necessity in the world of my imagination. I splashed myself copiously with Aqua Manda in the 1970s; it smelt of citrus and coriander, and came in a brown and orange packaging that chimed perfectly with the aesthetic of the time. Or there was Hungary Water, which smelt of bergamot and rosemary. When I wanted something stronger, I sometimes turned to the bright, aldehydic blue and silver of Rive Gauche (Jacques Polge, 1969). But when my first daughter was born, Yves St Laurent introduced Opium (Jean-Louis Sieuzac, 1977), which was a sort of landmark, warm and orangey-spicey but also complex and sophisticated, with the staying power of Estée

Lauder's Youth Dew. It was boxed in brown and gold, the bottle with a silk tassel and netsuke/inro-style referencing. For a long while I was completely sold on it. After Opium there was Dior's Poison (Edouard Flechier, 1985) which I found fascinating for a few months, but ultimately too metallic and aggressive.

Opium and Poison are often associated with the sexual politics of the 1980s. Psychologist and perfume specialist Joachim Mensing is regularly quoted as having declared that both were 'feminist fragrances', but whilst Opium was about introspection and self-discovery, Poison was about power in sexual politics. It came in a dark glass globe like 'a magic fruit filled with belladonna', suggesting magic, or 'a female fantasy of sexual domination'. Mensing was definitely on to something there. The 1980s and early 1990s were a troubled time for me, both emotionally and in the workplace.

I didn't care for the fruity/vanilla/marine perfumes of the 1990s. Instead, I explored my way through older scents, the perfume houses of Caron and Guerlain. Guerlain's Mitsouko and Parure were favourites. Mitsouko (Jacques Guerlain, 1919) had huge appeal: I got through many bottles of the stuff. I started to read about scent in more depth, becoming fascinated with the history of perfume and the extent to which marketing – and, related to this, concepts of desirable femininity – had shifted through time.

My daughters were growing up and it was a joy to discover that they learned to care as much about perfume as I did. We used to go around department stores together, comparing our reactions to various scents. We made special journeys to try out perfumes: regularly to L'Artisan Parfumeur (then with a branch in Chelsea) and to the South of France, to Italy, to Serge Lutens in the Palais Royale in Paris. The memory of each journey is enshrined in perfume; Molinard's Habanita from Grasse, L'Eau d'Italie from Positano. After my daughters left home this shared interest in scent brought us together on numerous occasions. One of them tells me that my father's, her grandfather's, choice of Dior's Fahrenheit cologne impacted on her reactions to young men at university; she tended to feel safe with anyone who smelled of this, often an unwarranted sense of security. Both daughters, to this day, give and ask for perfume as birthday presents, and we share discussions about scent as avidly as ever.

When Covid-19 struck in the UK, and through the various degrees of lockdown and limited travel that followed, I turned to thinking even more intensively about perfume. I ordered samples of essential oils, the smells of which were relatively unfamiliar to me: spikenard, frankincense, different kinds of tonka and oudh. And I focused on the history of perfume advertising, and how a detailed study of this could throw light on the social history of women's changing aspirations, their fantasies and dreams. I wrote an article about the subject, which was published in *History Today* (September 2020), under the title of 'Perfume, History, Dreams', emphasising the potent mix of memory and desire encapsulated in the history of scent. I found myself fascinated, further, by the associations between scent and social class, as well as between different ideas about gender in the past.

These associations between scent, social class and gender were rarely stable, and a great deal has depended on context and marketing. One of the most popular scents of the 1920s was Grossmith's Phūl-Nānā. It had been introduced in 1891, and the name allegedly translated from the Hindi as 'lovely flowers'. It was originally packaged with an image of a woman done up like a nautch girl, garlanded, loose-haired and wearing ankle bracelets, dancing in gay abandon. In some versions, an Indian prince, seated on a carpet, looked on. Phūl-Nānā was available in tiny bottles with red plastic tops, or in cachoux form, and you could buy it in corner shops or in Woolworths. It was ubiquitous, and often considered a bit vulgar. Writer and cultural theorist Richard Hoggart, who grew up in working-class Leeds, remembered an aunt who recoiled at the smell of Phūl-Nānā, saying it reminded her of 'fags and farts'. Another of his aunts, 'from a more genteel world', wore Lily of the Valley (Coty's Muguet des Bois, 1941, Henri Robert), which was thought 'classy', but never Phūl-Nānā, leaving Hoggart in no doubt that the scent 'would have been common, real Woolworths, even for us'.

There are many such references. Phūl-Nānā and its sister 'exotic' scents (Hasu-no-Hana, 1888, Shem-el-Nessim, 1906) gradually disappeared, and today's perfume lovers scan the internet looking for vintage examples. Grossmith introduced a new fragrance, White Fire, in 1954, which was packaged in a little red bottle, pleasure-dome shaped, like one of the turrets atop Brighton Pavilion. But the firm, which had originally been founded in 1835, had changed hands by 1970, and ceased trading altogether in 1980. Until some thirty years later when Simon Brooke, a descendant of the original founder of Grossmith, came across old leather-bound books containing the formulae for the original scents. With assistance from perfume expert Roja Dove, Brooke relaunched some of the original Grossmith fragrances. One can now buy Phūl-Nānā, Shem-el-Nessim and Hasu-no-Hana in high-end London department stores. They are expensive: near £300 for 100ml. No longer packaged in their characteristically oriental, high-colonial form (the original scent adverts tended to show white women being waited upon by brown-skinned servants, or inducted by houris into the secrets of the Orient), there is some irony in the fact that the revived fragrances are rumoured to appeal particularly to wealthy consumers from the Middle East.

Assumptions about desirable fragrances are closely bound up with gender. Ideals of femininity have shifted and changed in the West since the middle of the nineteenth century, a timespan during which 'modern' perfumery developed. In Victorian times, women were supposed to be modest and retiring. Young ladies were pictured leaning against or twining themselves around pillars of male strength, like ivy round oak trees. They were supposed to smell of flowers, especially delicate little fragrant ones like violets or lilies of the valley. Larger, more exotic, hothouse blooms – oleanders, orchids, gardenias, tuberose – did feature in perfume but were more risky, particularly if you wanted to appear innocent and unsullied. Botanical symbolism or the 'language of flowers' permeates Victorian painting and literature. In perfumery, 'single note' florals ('soliflores') dominated, with perfume houses like Zenobia, Breidenbach or the Crown Perfumery producing long lists of floral scents.

Orientalism made strides in perfumery around the turn of the century, with coded – and not so coded – references to sheiks, harem pants and sex appeal. Women started to smoke, and the fragrant fumes of incense and tobacco crept into the olfactory imagination in perfumes like Caron's Tabac Blond (Ernest Daltroff, 1917) and Molinard's Habanita (1921). Flappers, and a more daring image of femininity, appear in perfume advertising: women who drive cars, and dream of cruising on ocean liners, or of air travel. Perfume paid homage to the romance of aeroplanes and pioneer female aviators; Ernest Daltroff's En Avion for Caron in 1932, Guerlain's Vol de Nuit the following year. The postwar years saw something of a revival of 'traditional' models of femininity, with the popularity of Rochas Femme (1944) and Bal à Versailles (Jeanne Desprez, 1962). These fragrances chimed with the appeal of Dior's New Look. But perfumery was soon to show the impact of the Youthquake and a challenging of traditional gender concepts, with fragrances such as Yves St Laurent's Rive Gauche, or Revlon's Charlie. Charlie appeared in 1973, and advertisements for the scent celebrated a confident young girl in a trouser suit, striding across the streets of the city.

Perfume adverts reveal insights into changing concepts of

femininity but, more than this, they illuminate the evolving relation between the sexes, and aspects of gender politics. That wearing a particular fragrance might help to lure a mate was being openly acknowledged in adverts for popular scents in the 1940s. Both Bourjois' Soir de Paris and Atkinsons' Californian Poppy were advertised directly to women as scents which would attract a partner and romance. Soir de Paris adverts often depicted romantic trysts near the Eiffel Tower; Californian Poppy adverts went further, regularly depicting a young woman (frequently in service uniform) sinking into the arms of a chisel-jawed young man (often in service uniform, too). Patriotism thus gave a respectable air to lust and longing. But after the war, perfume advertising was as likely to address itself to men as to women: it was presumed that men would be the main buyers of scent, as Christmas presents for their girlfriends, wives and mothers.

Given that many men were expected to be clueless about scent, the adverts set out to make things easier for them. Coty excelled itself here. In an advert which appeared in the popular paper *Picture Post* in December 1954, it showed three men, bowler-hatted, pondering what gifts to get for their loved ones. The copy read:

> Look Chaps… About this perfume lark! Christmas. Presents for her. So, perfume. Why? Well, all women like perfume. Good perfume. Coty is good perfume. So far, so good. All you have to do now is suit the perfume to the woman. There are all types of women. Coty make all types of perfume. Here's how it works out…

There followed a series of questions about the characteristics of the female who the gift was intended for: was she 'magnetic'? If so, she should be given Coty L'Aimant. Was she a goddess? If so, she deserved L'Origan. If superstitious, she merited Muguet des Bois. And so on. This was actually a simplification of earlier versions of the Coty advert, which had provided would-be masculine givers of perfume with a detailed checklist of female personality types together with the kind of fragrance that was likely to appeal to them ('Is she a smart townswoman with instinctive poise and artistic talents? Give her Muse').

Other perfume houses followed in Coty's footsteps and introduced their own, often rather mind-boggling, schema. In the late 1940s, for instance, Jourdon True Charm perfumes were suggesting that women could be categorised into one of eight personality types with clear indications for what fragrance would elicit their 'TRUE personality and prove the RIGHT perfume to crystalise their natural allure'. The eight categories were effectively geographically based. There were supposedly women who went for 'Old English' scents, others more inclined to Hawaii, Monte Carlo, Araby or Manhattan. There was even a category for those with a 'Siberian' bent, whatever that may have implied.

After the 1950s, magazine adverts for women's perfumes directed at men as the potential purchasers continued, especially in the run-up to Christmas, but there was an increasing tendency to target women as buyers of their own scent. In women's magazines, particularly, readers were told that Frenchwomen wore fragrance every day, lamenting that the habit still had to catch on with English girls, who were wasting opportunities to increase their charms. Atkinsons latched on to this with an advert in cod French, with a French girl telling her English friend, 'But I am amazed! In France we say the English girls they are lovely, *mais quelle pitié*! ... no perfume!' (*Picture Post*, 1950). More women were going out to work and had the wherewithal to buy their own cosmetics and scent. And manufacturers facilitated this by selling perfume in tiny, inexpensive bottles, as Goya had since the 1940s, or by marketing and promoting scents through bath oil, as did

Estée Lauder with Youth Dew, this seeming less of a self-indulgence, maybe, than perfume proper. Towards the end of the twentieth century, women were far less shy of buying their own perfume, and marketing and advertising reflected this. In one notorious advert for Opium in 2000, model Sophie Dahl was photographed naked, her pale body stretched languorously against dark silk. Rather than dreaming of romance, she appeared to luxuriate in her own pleasure. The advert proved highly controversial, leading to an (unsuccessful) campaign to have it banned.

I have always understood scents and fragrances as part of getting dressed. The idea of a 'signature' scent remains foreign to me because fragrance is so intimately bound up with colour, clothing, context and mood. And because, as a historian, I recognise that there are changing fashions in perfume, and that these fashions are part of our social and cultural history, our material past, and also that they teach us something about the social history of the emotions. Perfumes haunt the imagination, fuelling memory with desire and the kind of longing which we sometimes recognise as nostalgia. Perfumer Olivia Giacobetti is on record as having suggested that perfume is a language close to the unconscious: its power remains in some degree mysterious, and like clothing, it can give out mixed messages. It is a rich and significant area of study for the social historian.

TWELVE

Adornment: Glitter, Poppets and Pearls

ONE OF MY EARLIEST REMEMBERED feelings of delight was when my grandmother allowed me to sift through the contents of her button tin. This was an old, round, yellow biscuit tin, heavy with its contents, which rattled promisingly as you levered off the lid. Inside was a treasure trove: buttons in all shapes and sizes, many in bright coloured glass or plastic, others pearly, iridescent, sparkly. There were some of particular gorgeousness: buttons in the shape of tiny teddy bears, a few with little images of Mickey Mouse and Muffin the Mule, some vintage 1920s buttons shaped like tiny scarab beetles, leaves, snowdrops and daisies. The tin held other treasures, too: tiny, milky porcelain dolls barely an inch long… I know now that these would have been 'Frozen Charlottes', popular in England and America from mid-Victorian times to the 1920s, often used as charms in Christmas puddings. I learned this only recently. As a child I did ask my mother and grandmother what they were, and what they were *for*, but don't remember ever getting an answer. I played with the idea of nestling them like Thumbelina in walnut shells.

My mother's jewellery collection was also a source of pleasure. There wasn't anything of significant value; my parents had very little money when I was a child, but there were pretty brooches and necklaces and the odd gold locket, discarded chains and watchstraps. And there were stories attached to several of these items. A smoky blue paste flower brooch with tin leaves, my mother told me, had been a present from her first boyfriend, who unfortunately had been caught shoplifting. A little green glass bauble in gold-coloured filigree swung from a decorative pin and had a tiny stopper so that you could fill it with perfume. And a fine gold chain with turquoise beads had been a christening present to me. Mum assured me that these three items were mine, and I have them still, although at one point, aged about five, I recall impulsively giving them away to a school friend who played at our house. She was called Stephanie and was much prettier than me, so I decided that she deserved them. Mum was furious, went round to explain to Stephanie's mum, and reclaimed them. I felt confused and ashamed, I remember.

My mother's and grandmother's jewellery collections were very much of their time. The 1950s were years of soaring demand for inexpensive costume jewellery, flowers and glitz, after the deprivations of wartime. Mitchel Maer designs for Dior, chunky necklaces and brooches by Trifari, multi-string pearls and diamante bracelets were not cheap but were widely copied: Adrian Mann and Exquisite offered less expensive versions. Charm bracelets were fashionable. Both my mother and my grandmother cherished theirs, buying tiny silver charms which as a child one was entranced by; parrots in cages, a cat with a mouse, a miniature teddy bear with jointed arms and legs, no more than half an inch long. More people were going abroad for their holidays and bringing back souvenirs. My grandmother bought tiny enamelled shields from the towns she visited, soldering these alongside the charms on her bracelet. Switzerland did a busy trade in brooches and earrings in the shape of gentians, edelweiss and narcissus. Originally carved out of bone, these were later crafted from plastics. Reverse carved Lucite brooches with flower designs were extremely popular in the 1940s and 1950s, with some women trying their hand at making their own. And there was a craze in the late 1950s for 'poppets', or plastic snap beads: they came pearlised or plain, in all the colours of the rainbow. You could accessorise any clothing with them and they cost very little. Many women – including my mother, and some of my friends – had heaps of them.

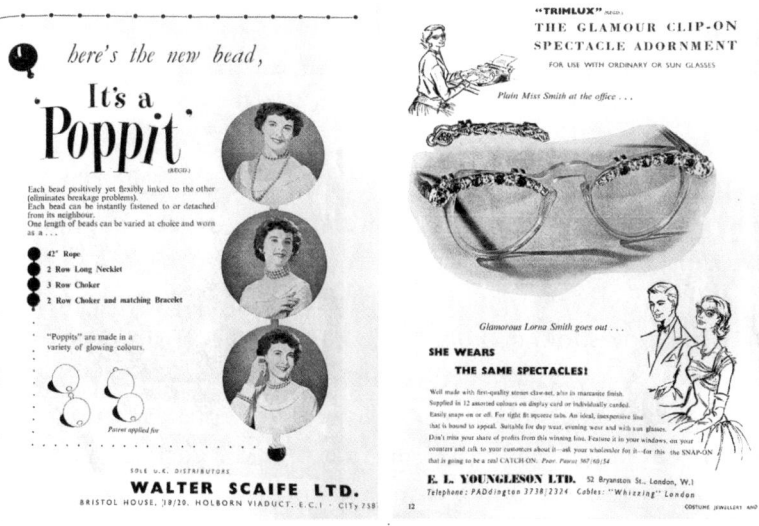

'Poppit' beads and twinkly spectacle adornments from the 1950s

As an adolescent I didn't bother much with jewellery, though, apart from the bits which had been handed down and had what was always called 'sentimental value'. Things changed a little at university. With friends, I spent time haunting antique and junk shops and developed an eye for pretty bits of Victoriana: beaded purses, the occasional old cut-glass perfume bottle, bits of jet. A boyfriend gave me a pretty Victorian chatelaine, and a delicate lacy necklace made from tiny jet and cut steel beads. Sadly, this broke. I salvaged most of the beads, and many years later, my younger daughter crafted them into a pretty friendship bracelet with a chevron design.

My interest in jewellery developed much later, whilst my children were growing up. I was writing about Victorian Britain in the 1970s and 1980s, and became curious about the symbolism of, and sentiment invested in, various aspects of 'feminine' culture and adornment. There was the language of flowers, for a start, which crept into perfume and decoration as well as other forms of fancy and romance. Lilies-of-the-valley and violets were demurely feminine, orchids and hothouse flowers quite other. Forget-me-nots were obviously about fidelity. Primroses had a purity about them; Prime Minister Disraeli, adored by Queen Victoria, allegedly claimed them his favourite flower. Victoria bombarded him with fat bunches of them. 'Primrose Day' was inaugurated in 1882, on the anniversary of Disraeli's death, marked by the widespread wearing of primroses across the country.

The Primrose League, with a mission to spread Conservatism in Britain, was founded one year later, in 1883. You can still find the little yellow enamelled primrose flower brooches in shops selling vintage, or at boot sales. Flowers were often recruited for social and political as well as decorative and romantic purposes. 'Snowdrop Bands', formed in Britain in the 1880s, aimed to protect factory girls from temptation and vice. Members of a Snowdrop Band carried a card embossed with snowdrops, signifying 'the white flower of a blameless life'. Round the borders were printed the words 'Let thy mind's sweetness have its operation on thy body, clothes and habitation'. The 'promise' on the back of the card committed members to 'discourage wrong conversation, light and immodest conduct and the reading of bad and foolish books'.

Gemstones, both valuable and semi-precious stones, also carried meaning. Diamonds stood for courage and strength; emeralds for foresight; garnets for constancy. The Victorians were fond of acrostic jewellery, where the initial letter of the name of each stone spelled out loving messages in settings read from right to left, such as 'Dearest' (Diamond, Emerald, Amethyst, Ruby, Emerald, Sapphire, Topaz), or 'Regard'. 'Mizpah' on a brooch stood for protection, a dedication taken from the Old Testament, meaning 'watchtower', and loosely interpreted as 'May God watch over you'. Jet jewellery was associated with mourning. Indeed, though the substance (a form of fossilised wood) had long been known and worked into ornaments from Roman times, the sudden rise of the jet industry in the coastal town of Whitby, in Yorkshire, was closely associated with Victorian practices and rituals of mourning. In 1832 there were two jet workshops in the town; in 1872, some 200. Queen Victoria's widowhood was an important factor: for many years jet jewellery was the only permitted form of adornment for ladies at court. Jet became extremely fashionable, and craftsmen highly skilled, turning out beads, lockets, bracelets and earrings in a wonderful variety of floral, abstract and intricately patterned designs. You could tenderly curl a lock of your deceased loved one's hair in a jet locket, fostering the feeling of him (or her) still being close to you in an intimate, physical sense. Or there was hair jewellery. The hair of departed loved ones could be delicately braided and tatted into a variety of intricate lacey shapes, acorns and tiny hollow cages, beads and chains.

The first time I encountered hair jewellery, it took me a while to realise what it was. It looked like brown lace. When it suddenly came to me that the lace was fashioned from human hair, I shuddered. But sensibilities change through time. Art historian Marcia Pointon has drawn attention to the several manuals of instruction published between the 1850s and 1870s, designed to skill young ladies in the craft of working in hair.

Jet, on the other hand, is delightful: lightweight, and when polished, creamy to the touch. Some of the bigger Victorian jet chains and drooping, bulky earrings are difficult to wear today but not so the brooches, bracelets and more delicate necklaces and collars. I developed an interest in jet jewellery towards the end of the last century. Its different textures when carved, its glossiness, appealed. And I've always been a bit of a goth. I liked wearing something from history. There's a problem though, in that jet breaks easily if you drop it. I feel guilt at having destroyed more than one pair of exquisitely carved earrings. Jet substitutes, such as 'French jet' (glass), bog oak and Vulcanite, are more durable. But Vulcanite – a form of rubber – fades to brown through time. The Victorians knew what they were doing when they developed a passion for jet.

Cut steel was another kind of jewellery which I was drawn to. It had a subtle glitter, not unlike, though to my mind much superior to, marcasite. Both looked great worn on black. Cut steel has a rarity value. It was made in the UK from the eighteenth century to the 1930s, consisting of polished and faceted steel studs riveted into a metal baseplate. It can rust easily and isn't easy to clean, which is one of the reasons why it can be hard to get hold of. Shoe buckles are the easiest to find, and it is wonderful to imagine all the twinkling toes of the past. Cut steel catches the light and sparkles beguilingly in candlelight.

I've never spent much on vintage jewellery. Jet still turns up in car boot sales and junk shops. The really beautiful, elaborate pieces can be expensive though, and I don't go for them. Ditto with cut steel. I have several pieces which I've paid very little for, having come across them in vintage market stores and second-hand shops over the years. Internet sites such as Etsy and ebay do foster temptation: it is hard to resist just idling away time, seeing what's out there. I've recently developed a liking for those brooches in the shape of edelweiss or narcissus, carved originally from cow bone, later made from early plastics. But I'm not really a collector. I buy things which I will mostly wear, and not worry too much about if I lose them. Loss is not uncommon, when brooches are old and have bent or less than perfect fastenings, and earrings so easily get caught in scarves and go astray.

Why do I find jewellery so fascinating? Traditionally, owning a few valuable bits and pieces was important to women, one of the main sources of their private wealth at a time when what they 'owned', if married, was deemed to belong to their husbands, and women were excluded from, or found it hard to access, financial institutions and structures. Jewellery might be part of a dowry. Or it might be bestowed on women when marrying into families with inherited wealth, although the 'ownership' of such might mean a temporary custodianship, in that the jewels were often regarded as belonging to the family and were not to be sold. Jewellery was portable: women fleeing from abusive or unhappy relationships might take it with them, as a first resource for survival.

The kind of jewellery which interests me most is not the expensive, precious kind. Costume jewellery and other forms of ornamentation can provide fascinating insights into women's changing dreams and aspirations, into ideas about class and gender, and expectations of different forms of femininity. In modern times, flicking through the jewellery adverts in girls' and women's magazines can be a richly rewarding business for the social and cultural historian. Here one can reimagine the outlook of a middle-aged lady of the shires (*Vogue*'s Mrs Exeter, perhaps), as her eye roved over adverts for marcasite brooches in the shape of pheasants, partridges, grouse and fox heads, just the thing to set off, and give class to, a nubbly tweed coat or jacket.

From a present-day perspective, these might seem less disturbing than the vintage Scottish kilt-pin-type of brooch, where a scaly talon or hooked bird claw (grouse or ptarmigan) would be garnished with an amethyst or topaz and collared and set in silver. But the cultural associations are not dissimilar. Or we might consider the endless advertisements for cheap engagement rings which proliferated in comics and magazines aimed at young teenage girls, papers such as *Romeo*, *Valentine*, *Marilyn* and *Boyfriend* in the 1950s and 1960s. These adverts reflect the sharp fall in the age of marriage after the Second World War and bear testimony to many girls' fears that they would be 'left on the shelf' if they failed to capture a husband before they arrived at the ripe old age of twenty-one.

A great deal has been written about the cultural history of pearls, but there is more to learn from their fashionableness and status as objects of desire among girls and women in the twentieth century. Pearls have long signified purity and a particular kind of refined femininity. Both pearl chokers and long ropes of pearls were worn by Queen Alexandra in the 1900s. Coco Chanel liked to wear masses of faux pearls, twining several ropes around her neck at the same time. A widely circulated image of screen siren Louise Brooks in the 1920s, wearing a long strand of pearls, looked edgy and modern. And somewhat later still, in 1961, Audrey Hepburn in *Breakfast at Tiffany's* wore a legendary black Givenchy dress set off by a collar of multi-stranded, outsize pearls.

Pearls indicated class, as much as glamour. As women's power as consumers increased in the early twentieth century and particularly after the Second World War, there can be no doubt that many of them hankered after pearls. A number of firms set out to meet this demand, marketing comparatively inexpensive faux pearl necklaces: Ciro, Monet and Rosita were almost household names, and there were also Elizabethan, Lotus, Corocraft and Samuel Jones. Some Rosita pearls came nestled in a satin-lined heart or scallop-shell shaped box. Simulated pearls often came with 'a certificate', attesting to quality. Faux pearls were heavily marketed in women's and girls' magazines between the 1930s and the 1960s, almost a badge of respectable femininity, and they were hugely popular, especially as gifts. Many young women aspired to marry in them. At the bottom of the range were plastic, pearlised poppets.

Pearls were a staple of what we might call the paraphernalia of femininity, especially in the 1950s and 1960s. These were decades which saw a burgeoning production both of costume jewellery and of other forms of glittery knick-knackery aimed at women. There were lipstick cases encrusted with fake gems, elaborate powder compacts by Stratton or Kigu, enamelled, jewelled, and even musical ones that played a tune as you lifted the lid to dab away the shine from your nose. There were sparkly, jewelled cigarette holders. One London firm (Trimlux) marketed clip-on spectacle adornments garnished with a row of claw-set stones or twinkly marcasite so that 'Plain Miss Smith at the office' could transmogrify herself into a glamorous sophisticate at night.

THIRTEEN

Adornment: Make-Up

I HESITATED OVER the naming of this section: should I entitle it 'Cosmetics' or 'Make-Up'? Cosmetics is the wider term: it might include perfume, nail varnish, as well as what are sometimes called 'grooming products': soap, shampoo, hairspray, deodorant, toothpaste, etcetera. The term 'grooming products' is horrid, and brings to mind horses. I like 'make-up', whether one or two words, with or without a hyphen. I don't mind the suggestion of artificiality. There's a long tradition of concern over such, of course. But ideas about face-painting as the preserve of 'lewd and wicked women' on the make failed to stem such practices in earlier centuries, and whatever one's prejudices, since the Second World War the use of cosmetics on a daily basis has become culturally normative in the UK.

Many young women were confidently making up their faces in the 1930s, eschewing any suggestion that it ill-befitted a lady to use more than a touch of vanishing cream, powder and – maybe – discreetly pale pink lipstick. Daughters often clashed with their mothers over these issues, and husbands weren't always tolerant of wives 'drawing attention to themselves' with cosmetics. Sharp-eyed Mass Observers, though, haunting London's East End, reported on girls hanging round 'the toilet counter' in Woolworths, investigating the latest shades of hair dye, pressed powder, lipstick and eyeshadow: girls were said to start using lipstick as early as thirteen years of age.

My grandmother kept a frosted, peachy-pink, pressed glass powder-bowl on her dressing table, topped with a satin and swansdown puff, but I think it was mainly for decoration. I don't remember her wearing make-up, though, apart from pressed powder and a hint of lipstick, but every day my mother used liquid foundation (Revlon) and a touch of rouge (Bourjois Rosette Brune, in a cute little blue-and-gold circular cardboard box). When she went out, she added lipstick, and mascara from one of those little plastic cases which contained a block of it, with a tiny brush. (You spat on the block mascara to apply it with the brush.)

I can't recall exactly when I started wearing cosmetics, which were of course strictly banned at secondary school. I think it was spots which started me off. I needed to conceal my adolescent pimples and resorted, like many of my peers, to Clearasil. This was a little too orange in colour, and I soon gravitated to Max Factor pancake or pan-stick make-up, which felt like a godsend. Dad being a pharmacist encouraged my interest in cosmetics, though the messages I got from him were contradictory. He was interested in the products he sold (including perfume) and yet became very critical when I tried too many of them out and started to look, in his eyes, 'tarty' or 'cheap'. Such a narrow line!

I remember that somewhere around adolescence we were asked, at school, for suggestions for topics of general interest with a practical bent and I suggested make-up. One of Dad's young female shop assistants had been on some kind of course organised by one of the big cosmetic houses (Elizabeth Arden? Yardley?) and I thought it would be fun if she came and talked to the Lower Sixth. Everyone liked the idea and so along she came, together with big bags of free samples. But tastes were changing in the early 1960s, against a backdrop of the Teenage

Revolution. Dad's assistant won the approval of the trendier teachers (a rather small proportion of the staff, most espousing the views of seventeenth-century Puritans), by emphasising the value of squeaky-clean skin ('Cleanse! Tone! Nourish!'), a rosebud mouth and a barely detectable trace of blue eyeshadow. But increasingly, like some of my peers, I aspired to heavy, smoky eye make-up, false eyelashes, and whited-out lips thick with Miners' 'Babydoll Peach' or some kind of milky almond pink by Outdoor Girl. Yardley and Elizabeth Arden were for good girls, debs and sissies.

I do remember a feeling of relief that you could change what you looked like through the careful use of cosmetics. I didn't like the way I looked 'naturally', so experimented enthusiastically with hair dyes, colours and creams. I think I used Clairol, or L'Oreal 'Color Glo', or similar semi-permanent tints, trying to make my weedy, mousy hair look more interesting, opting first for auburn tints, then dark chocolate. There was a short-lived experiment with a shade that I think was called 'Black Tulip' which attracted disapproval at home and school. My mother complained about rings of colour round the basin and what I was doing to all the bath towels. Then I discovered Richard Hudnut 'Light and Bright' which you just combed in for blonde highlights and it seemed to look better, so I stuck with it for a while. As for lipstick and eye make-up, I did buy some things from Woolworths like all my friends, but Dad's pharmacy was an endless source of free samples. There was such poetry in the names of the lipsticks of the 1950s: Revlon's legendary 'Fire and Ice' and 'Cherries in the Snow'. But these were reds, and for mothers and aunts. For the newer, paler colours, one went elsewhere. I spent many evenings with my friend Jayne, sitting on her bedroom floor listening to records and trying stuff on: pale pink and chalky peach lipsticks from Woolworths, Miners or Outdoor Girl, and green or mauve eyeshadow.

This pattern of sharing cosmetics and learning about different ways of making up continued through university, where evenings were often spent in each other's 'study bedrooms', gossiping, dressmaking, drinking tea and – regrettably – smoking. Not quite 'Friday Night is Amami Night', but there was a lot of female bonding. We did each other's hair. Many of us experimented with false hairpieces and upswept styles, then fashionable, sometimes with daisies poked into the curls and the whole ensemble pinned and heavily lacquered. Looking back, this tended to make us look like elaborate knickerbocker glories. For special nights out, we spoke of 'getting tarted up', and pooled advice: even, sometimes, clothes. After leaving university I spent short periods school-teaching. There was a shaming moment, in one period of teaching practice, when the deputy head took me aside and accused me of wearing too-short skirts and too much eye make-up. It was a relief to get back to university as a graduate student and to have no-one tell me how to look.

Except that graduate studies and the first years of paid employment coincided, for me, with the rise of second-wave feminism: I was enthusiastic. I eagerly anticipated every new issue of *Spare Rib*, and my bookshelves filled up with green-backed editions of Virago. Feminism helped clarify why I'd always resented double standards at home, and where my brothers were concerned; it also provided valuable insights into all the sexism patently obvious at work. But many feminists cast a disapproving eye over cosmetics and make-up. Should one really worry about hairy legs? Was it a mark of pusillanimity to refuse to go out without make-up? I wrestled with these ideas for a short while but eventually decided to carry on regardless. Later, studying the relationship between feminism and glamour, I learned more about the complexities. The historical context in which cosmetics were and are used has always been important. In spite of sneers over 'lipstick feminists', bright red lipstick *was* and still can be read as a sign of confidence and self-assertion. And the enthusiastic hair blonding, brow-plucking and face painting of women 'screen goddesses' in the heyday of Hollywood cinema was regularly construed as bold or 'forward'. The relationship between 'nature' and 'artifice' is rarely one of contrasting absolutes: the 'natural' look of the 1970s sometimes took a great deal of skill and calculation.

The quality of cosmetics and toiletries has vastly improved since the middle of the last century. In the 1950s, for instance, there was little in the way of hair conditioner. Girls' magazines still recommended ruses such as rubbing beaten egg yolks through the hair after washing. If the water used was too hot, there was a danger of having to comb out lumps of scrambled egg. Lemon juice and beer rinses allegedly added body and shine, but the beer rinses made you smell like a brewery. There was a beer shampoo called Linc-o-Lin. Lemon juice, egg whites and cucumber were supposed to improve skin. Bad skin meant misery for countless adolescents: one of my brothers used to swab his face with surgical spirit or even lighter fuel. Foundation creams and powders generally came in a couple of shades, 'Fair' (pinkish) and 'Rachel' (darker, a kind of light tan). Eventually, in the 1950s, the cosmetics house Gala advertised a new shade of beige, which it called 'Mutation Mink', playing on women's desire for fur coats in that decade. Anti-perspirants and deodorants were primitive immediately after the Second World War (Odorono), and young women were often anxious about underarm sweating. The pop group, *The Who*, recorded a song about Odorono, focusing on a girl who lost her lover on account of her smelly armpits.

The history of the naming, packaging and advertising of cosmetics offers many insights into cultural and social change. Some of the adverts common in the early twentieth century had been brutal; playing on girls' fear of smelly armpits, bad breath and social rejection. They had lauded 'daintiness', a word extremely common at the time, often a proxy word for cleanliness or hygiene. Magazines had regularly featured adverts for chin reducers and nose straps. The *Daily Mail* 'Beauty Book' recommended 'Veedee Vibrators', as allegedly used by the Duchess of Argyll and various other aristos; these, it claimed, reduced wrinkles and excess flesh. This book had also recommended an 'anti-fat mixture' containing spirits of ammonia and 'iodide of potash'. Gradually, the hortatory and scary tone of cosmetic advertising gave way to self-care and pleasure. The careers of cosmetics duennas Elizabeth Arden and Helena Rubinstein illustrate something of this, although both saw beauty, additionally, as something of a moral imperative, and the tone of their recommendations could be quite severe. Quite late in the interwar period, Helena Rubinstein was recommending a beauty mask made from slices of raw beef.

By 1958 most women in the UK were using cosmetics: a survey of 'Modern Cosmetics and Perfumery' by the research organisation Political and Economic Planning, which was published in that year, emphasised the lessons of wartime: cosmetics raised morale, it stated, and the government should take the industry seriously. Exports of British-made cosmetics to the Commonwealth countries and Europe were worth some £8 million per annum. At home, the average woman over fifteen years of age was spending around £3 per annum on cosmetics. Three out of four women wore face powder and lipstick, whilst nail varnish and eye make-up were rapidly gaining popularity among the young.

The impact of the Youthquake of the 1960s was profound. Cosmetics began to be marketed as fun, as playthings. Adverts became suggestive of experimenting with finger paints, rather than hawking the bejewelled, sophisticated lipstick-and-compact cases so appealing to their parents' generation. Woolworths' new 'Baby Doll' range flaunted psychedelic graphics to advertise 'a fab new range of shiny makeup… in

Woolworth's 'Baby Doll' cosmetics, 1960s

colours that will really grab you' and in either 'sunshiny' or 'moonshiny' tones. There was often a decidedly regressive tone to this. Mary Quant advertised her 'Jelly Babies' range in baby-bottle-shaped containers with teat-shaped tops. Adverts for cosmetics and 'fun' make-up appeared in all the newer magazines widely devoured by young girls; *Rave*, *Honey* and of course *Jackie*. Girls were encouraged to stick diamante spots under their eyes and to experiment with false eyelashes. The naming of colourways became ever more playful, setting the scene for the launching of punk-inspired cosmetic lines (such as Urban Decay or Hard Candy) later in the century. 'Stray Dog Eye Pencil', 'Asphyxia Lip Gunk' and Soap & Glory's 'Sexy Mother Pucker Lip Gloss' or 'Glow Job Foundation' were a long way away from 'Cherries in the Snow'.

The cupboards in my bathroom today are crammed full of hair and beauty products, creams and lotions, bath essences and scented soaps. And several drawers and surfaces in my bedroom groan under the weight of cosmetics. I think ruefully of Angela Carter's descriptions of Fevvers, the winged woman circus performer in her novel *Nights at the Circus*, sitting before 'the formidable refuse' of her dressing table. I have sometimes felt guilty about all this stuff, though if I'm honest, this is usually in connection with anyone seeing the pile-up for the first time. The collection tends to get dusty with loose powder… and dust. I am not going to count the number of lipsticks or palettes of eye colour, but the number is very large. There must be twenty kinds of black eyeliner at least: kohl, liquid liner, various ink pens, pencils, gel-creams. And all those different-coloured nail varnishes, whole shoe boxes full of them, accumulated over the last couple of decades and more. They last a long time, I find. You're not supposed to keep old make-up, but I do, of course. I've still got a Biba eyeshadow in its distinctive little black and gold pot. I did throw out the liver and dark intestine-coloured lipsticks so fashionable at the end of the last century. In retrospect, they made us look a bit too much like Coleridge's Nightmare Life-in-Death who 'thicks man's blood with cold'.

So many of these pigments and potions enshrine memories. Biba, for instance, used to offer eyeshadows and lipsticks in shades of khaki, plum and burgundy, the colour of bruises or dark fruit. Chanel nail varnish in Rouge Noir (Vamp) was extremely hard to get hold of when it first came out in the 1990s; everyone wanted it. On holiday with my daughters, we combed New York department stores for bottles, my husband (their father) sighing with incomprehension at the intensity of the quest. More recently, we've hankered after discontinued perfumes: Guerlain's Après L'Ondée, smelling of hawthorn and wet violets, L'Artisan Parfumeur's Dzing!, with its inimitable circussy, animal scent. Alex once tracked down a bottle of Coty's legendary L'Origan (1905) on the internet; we couldn't wait to sample this, acknowledged as a turning point in the history of perfume.

Painting our faces has always been a point of pooled experience between me and my daughters, a form of bonding. In the past, when going out, we would vie for space before a large bathroom mirror where the light was perfect. My younger daughter, an engineer, is particularly skilled at using cosmetics to create historical and theatrical looks. There was ever a great deal of teasing, but also the sharing of knowledge. I look back on those times with pleasure.

So: I need to throw out old make-up and cosmetics along with my blitz on the wardrobes. I can't kid myself into thinking I need it all for reference anymore. But will I stop desiring and buying? There's a big tangle of worry about labour conditions, monopolies, plastics, ecology, climate change, of course. But there is also so much enjoyment bound up with the sensuousness of creams and potions, their scent, sometimes exquisite packaging, the feel and the promise of transformation. More than fifty years ago, American writer Eve Merriam poured scorn on the idea of miracle creams in her brilliantly penetrating study of the postwar fashion industry, *Figleaf*. Women were so easily gulled into falling for creams and jellies, the latest hormone-based, youth-inducing formula: 'oil of pure hogwash', she scoffed, would always sell. When historian Kathy Peiss published her history of American beauty culture in 1998, she entitled it *Hope in a Jar*. And perhaps that's what it is. Where there's life, there's hope. But also, pleasure, present and remembered. I still regret having used up Shiseido's brilliant 'Three Blacks' eye palette, more than two decades ago. It contained three different textures of black shadow, and came in a glossy, oval case. But web searches have revealed a more recent offering, by the same Japanese, Tokyo-based company. It is a black shadow with a 'powdergel' formula, and it comes in a wafer-thin black compact with an elegant red edge stripe, complete with mirror in lid, and is a delight.

FOURTEEN

My Mother's Clothes, and her Mother's

MY MOTHER'S CLOTHES were neat: she prided herself on her neatness. Indeed, she told me several times that as a pupil at St Thomas's Elementary School in Birmingham in the 1930s, she had been awarded a prize for that very quality. I have it still: a book inscribed 'to Connie B., for neatness'. Mum boasted that her teachers had entrusted her with bringing tea trays to the staffroom in the afternoons on account of her domestic skills. She was regularly excused lessons for the purpose. So much for the values of education for girls in the 1930s: neatness, needlework and domestic economy were seen as quintessentially feminine, and they very much mattered. Mum had been competent at arithmetic, but what she boasted of were her neat columns of figures, the careful display of 'workings out'. Somehow, she still passed her entrance examination for grammar school, but left early 'on account of the war'. One day she and her friends had arrived at the school gates to find heaps of rubble and serious bomb damage to the classrooms. Mum told me that they had all cheered.

My mother's family would have seen themselves as respectable working class. An ordered household was central to respectability, especially in the back-to-back terraces of central Birmingham. Homes were crowded, with shared outside lavatories, but the children were sent to school in

CHAPTER FOURTEEN

My grandmother as a young woman,
outside her shop in Small Heath, Birmingham, 1920s

polished shoes and clean clothes. Grandad was a leather worker. My grandmother had social aspirations. After she married Grandad, she set herself up as a shopkeeper in Green Lane, Small Heath. I have a photo of her proudly standing in the doorway. It is a small general store, with prominent adverts for Cadbury's chocolates. Posters advertising a couple of films (*Fighting the Flames* and *Too Many Kisses*) date the photo to around 1925. My grandmother also took in lodgers, finding ways of earning money alongside bringing up three children. Later, in her fifties, she went out charring for the local dentist's wife. The two women took to each other, and the dentist's wife promoted her to a kind of lady companion. Leaving the dentist and my grandfather behind, they embarked on a series of trips abroad, working their way round the Italian Riviera. On their returning from these trips, I was always given a

My grandmother, early 1950s (left); contemporary magazine advert for similar outfit (right)

souvenir doll. I remember one with blonde plaits and a raffia skirt across which was written on the slant, 'Cattolica'.

My grandmother, by the time I knew her, dressed extremely well. Photos show her in snazzy tailored costumes, or Horrockses-style sundresses with high-heeled, peep-toed shoes. She carried gloves, and classy handbags. Some of the classy handbags must have come from the factory where Grandad worked. One, in crocodile skin the colour of horse chestnuts, I have still. The handbags were lined either in soft suede or in a lovely sturdy watered silk. My grandmother used to fashion dolls' clothes for me as a child, out of the silk lining material.

I am reminded of Carolyn Steedman's memoir of growing up, *Landscape for a Good Woman*. Steedman emphasised the importance of clothes in working-class women's dreams of social betterment. Dressing well could be a source of self-respect but it could also help you to pass as being of a higher social standing than others might accord you. Steedman remembered that as a child she had wondered what social class she and her family belonged to: she thought they must be middle class because her mother looked so good in her 'black waisted coat with the astrakhan collar, and her high-heeled black suede shoes, her lipstick': she looked so much better than 'the fat, spreading South London mothers around us, that I thought we had to be middle class'. The 'cut and fall of a skirt and good leather shoes' were a defence, a route to respectability: clothes, shoes, make-up were 'the material stepping stones' of women's imagined escape from the working class.

When my grandmother died, she left drawers full of twinsets in soft Merino wool, and many pairs of gloves in kid or suede, in wine-gummy colours: bottle green, dark blue, magenta. Many of her clothes were unworn. I think she hoarded things 'for best', or so that she would feel safe and not run out. She hadn't always been able to afford nice things. In the photo of her standing outside the shop in Small Heath in the 1920s, she's wearing very shabby clothes.

My mother married at eighteen – not at all unusual in those days. She always said that what she had wanted most in life was a nice home and four children. She achieved this by marrying my father, the kind of young man of promise, who, even with a working-class background, was clearly destined to do well. Dad was an energetic, generous and ambitious man, romantically drawn to my mother, I think, by her somewhat shy, unambiguous femininity. They shared the desire for a family life with clear, gendered role expectations. Dad liked Mum to stay at home. It accentuated his role as provider. His favourite TV character was 'Katie', played by actress Mary Holland in the OXO adverts. Katie was given to sharing tips about how to crumble OXO cubes into her husband Philip's gravy because he liked it 'rich and meaty', and because 'OXO gives a meal man-appeal'. I thought she was creepy, but Dad used to confess that he found her altogether lovely and I don't think he was joking. Through most of their lives, even after Dad turned himself into a successful entrepreneur and businessman, he went home to have his lunch, cooked by Mum. However conflicted my parents' relationships became, in later years, I'm pretty sure that neither of them would ever have questioned the assumptions about gender roles on which their marriage was premised.

My mother as a young woman

Mum's clothes were always feminine and understated. She didn't go in for the touches of flamboyancy evident in some of the photographs of my grandmother. She dressed mostly in pleated skirts and pastel-coloured twinsets. Over these she wore frilled cotton aprons during the day. Just like the stereotype of the 1950s housewife. The aprons were the kind tied round the waist, often brightly patterned in yellow and red designs which matched the kitchen décor. She and Dad did the kitchen up like a flower shop or fairground stall, with red-and-white striped 'pelmets' and cheerful fabrics which they would have referred to as of a 'contemporary' pattern. Mum sometimes exchanged her aprons for pale blue nylon button-through overalls of the kind worn by women assistants in my father's chemist's shop. I think it must have made her feel more professional about her housework. She did an awful lot of housework, all day, every day. Later, it was in the spirit of being driven. The house was always as neat as a pin. I grew up refusing to wear an apron, and always avoided them. When, shortly after my own wedding, I was sent one as a present, I quietly shoved it in the bin.

Stuck at home with young children, Mum joined something called The Young Wives group, which operated locally. They shared discussions and tea and cake. I don't think anything like a whiff of feminism intruded. It didn't last long, anyway, they were all too busy with housework. Mum had very little leisure. Occasionally she and Dad would go to 'dinner dances'; I'm not sure how these were organised, or who organised them. Some may have been connected with my father's membership of Rotary. Much the most interesting of Mum's dresses in the 1950s were bought with these dinner dances in mind. I remember four of them: they were all full skirted, with stiff petticoats bolstering the crinoline effect. The length was mid-calf and she wore them with peep-toed, high-heeled shoes. One was in black and white, mainly in fine black cotton, with a white broderie anglaise insert in the bodice. The tuxedo effect this created was set off with a little black velvet ribbon necktie. Another dress was coffee-coloured lace, lined with a darker shade of taffeta. The third was lemon-sherbet yellow, very froufrou, strapless with a ruched bodice. The fourth dress which comes to mind was probably the most interesting and I only have a vague picture in my mind of her wearing it. I think it was earlier than the others. It was apricot-coloured, verging on coral, with a halter neckline and the skirt was full of sharp 'Sunray' pleats. In retrospect, I can see that it bore more than a passing resemblance to the dress designed by William Travilla for Marilyn Monroe in *The Seven Year Itch* (1955). I think it was the most glamorous dress that Mum ever owned, and wish I could remember exactly when she wore it. These dresses called for Playtex girdles, elasticated roll-on underwear to accentuate the waspy waists. Mum was a great believer in the roll-on girdle. When I hit adolescence she assumed that I'd wear one; otherwise, she warned, my flesh would run out of control and I'd grow up sagging.

Mum's style of dress didn't change all that much through time: she went on looking neat and well groomed most of the time, with just the occasional evening foray into glamour. But there were slight touches of more panache in the early sixties. This was influenced in the first place by Dad buying her a motor scooter, a Vespa, on which she would whizz down to the local shops wearing a stripey top and sunglasses. When she learned to drive a car, the Vespa found a new home; it didn't last all that long. Then there was the impact of package holidays abroad, much enjoyed by my parents, who regularly lugged the whole family round European resorts, and finally, as Dad's businesses and income grew, to exotic locations much further afield. Photos from the 1960s show Mum adopting touches of Riviera chic: sundresses, chunky necklaces and a multitude of swimming costumes. These last she would accessorise with bathing hats covered all over with rubber-petalled flowers to protect her hair.

My mother's day clothes rarely strayed to sexy, though; there was nothing really daring or revealing of her (very good) figure. As a teenager, I inevitably compared her style with that of some of my friends' mothers. She always (until her sad, final illness) looked young and fresh and, yes, neat. Usually a bit housewifey, bordering on school secretary, apart from those late 1950s dinner-dance dresses. Unlike my close friend Jayne's mum, who had a much racier style. Jayne's mum wore tight black polo neck sweaters and slim pencil skirts. She peroxided her hair and wore it up in a smooth French pleat, with large hoop or dangling earrings. (My own mother's earrings were generally small silver leaves or little pearls.) Jayne's mum and her husband were keen amateur theatricals. They smoked and they drank. (My own mother's drinking rarely strayed past the odd Cherry B., Babycham or at Christmas, maybe, a 'snowball' laced with Advocaat.) Jayne's mum didn't seem too fussed about housework. I used to sit in Jayne's bedroom and we tried out make-up while we listened to the Beatles on Jayne's Dansette record player and talked about ponies, pop music and periods. Mum was always a bit wary of Jayne's parents' style. But to me, Jayne's mum was intriguing. There was her touch of exoticism, a suggestion of glamour, a certain sophistication about men and the world. And she always seemed so relaxed about untidy bedrooms and things.

I realise now that style posed all sorts of difficulties for working-class women, especially those bent on bettering themselves whilst holding on to reputation. Before marriage, it could pay to look neat and demure, not to look too 'fast' or challenging to men. Feminine neatness signified respectability, a form of self-containment or continence, the right kind of moral values. Messy women with slatternly habits wouldn't look like a safe bet for domestic comfort or harmony, and – worse – they might have relaxed morals, too. My father would have been uneasy about glamour, or anything he would have seen as too 'showy' in a woman. He was a grammar school boy from a working-class home with powerful ambitions to make something of himself. Part of this project would have been to look for a wife who would support him in every way, someone who (like Katie in the OXO ads) would dress prettily, cook him nourishing stews, have neat domestic habits and create a warm home.

Much later in my life I met up with Jayne as an adult; we were both parents ourselves by then. I confessed that I had always slightly envied her mother. Jayne laughed and said that she had often felt the same about mine. My mum had always seemed homely and reassuring to her. It was hard for women to get things right in the 1950s.

FIFTEEN

Daughters: Memories, Threads

My daughters, Alex and Eugénie von Tunzelmann, are grown up now, adults in their forties. Alex, the elder, is a writer and historian. Eugénie is an engineer and computer graphics artist who has worked in film and now specialises in theme park rides. They've both always seemed to have more confidence in themselves than I had, although because I want this for them, there may be an element of wishful thinking here. I don't think that they've had a history of agonising over what they wear in the way I have, and their wardrobes, I fancy, are far less stuffed. But both women are stylish, and care about how they look. I wanted to explore the development of their interest in clothes and to try to understand something of formative influences, memories and common threads. Where possible I shall use their own words, quoting from what they wrote for me.

I asked about their memories of clothes in childhood, what they recall liking and disliking. Both remembered the colour and *feel* of some of their early garments:

> The key memories I have from this time are more about feel than look. The only thing I really hated, that you'd try to dress me in, was wool. I still hate it. Feels like hundreds of tiny needles to me and makes my eczema flare up – even merino. [EvT]

> As a young child, I had strong feelings about colour. I had an ice blue velour tracksuit which I adored. I also loved pink and purple combinations: I remember some striped socks that were pink and purple. I also loved an olive green zip-up corduroy jumpsuit because I thought it made me look like a dinosaur. I think I was far less invested in textures than Eugénie, though I do remember liking a big fake fur coat, and chewing the sleeve which was for some reason extremely tasty. [AvT]

Eugénie also remembered the colour and feel of a satiny dress: here, her memory was probably reinforced by the existence of a photo of her wearing it. She also remembered that I had drawn the dress for her before buying it: I was concerned to involve them in decisions about what they wore, not just to project my fantasies on them.

> I remember a white and tan satin dress, with fine diagonal stripes, that you got me – I think I'm wearing it in a photo maybe? – and I distinctly remember you drawing it for me first, before buying it, after you'd spotted it in a shop. I loved it. I don't remember a lot more than that. [EvT]

The girls picked up on the fact that I cared about clothes, but they certainly learned that their father didn't, so there were two perspectives on apparel at home. Alex writes:

> I was always extremely aware that my mother adored and valued clothes and my father couldn't have had less interest. So I think clothes presented a specific bonding opportunity with my mother. This could take the form of coveting the same things – I loved sparkle – or ridiculing things that didn't seem to work, like that godawful orange bobbly jumper. We were so vicious about it! But I also know we

could bring it up now and all laugh about it because it was a shared moment. We would also all take the mickey out of my father's clothes because they were often so thoughtlessly selected... He took it very well. I think he took a certain intellectual pride in not giving a damn about clothes.

Our daughters, Alex and Eugénie, with their father, Nick von Tunzelmann, 1990s

I might have tried, as a parent, not to foist my own choices onto my children, but didn't always get it right. Peer group influences were strong and judgemental once the girls started school. Eugénie remembers her early school experiences:

> I don't remember having very strong feelings about look, but I do know that sometimes you'd dress me in retro stuff (hand-me-downs or hand-makes) and I'd think it was pretty, but school friends would take the piss. Little fuckers. [EvT]

It wasn't long before these peer group pressures intensified. I asked when the girls became aware of these pressures really kicking in. Eugénie recalled:

> Pretty young I think, maybe eight or nine. I didn't share most of the kids' tastes when it came to pop culture, but I was aware that a certain modern, premature-teen look (hoodies, tracksuit bottoms, trainers, crop tops) had started dominating over what I was often wearing (think 1970s dresses with hand embroidery, corduroy, quilted jackets) and I felt the need to start moving into that world. Partially it was to avoid the piss being taken and partially it was about keenness to move from childhood to teenage status. Honestly, I never really loved the teen look, but I did love feeling a bit more mature.
>   There was more open piss-taking from peers in my early teenage years. I put on warm tights one year and someone in the changing rooms said, 'Eugenie's got woolly baby tights!' and everybody laughed. I hadn't really considered that the sexiness of winter tights was worth considering. I stopped wearing them, though. (I wear them now, mind.) [EvT]

Alex remembered peer group and pop cultural influences intruding strongly in her early teens:

> I have such a specific memory about this from when I was about thirteen. I was at an after-school acting class. We did the classes in our own clothes, not school uniform. I was wearing jeans and an M&S t-shirt which had a design

embroidered on it in beads and sequins that featured various snack products: fizzy drinks, burgers, crisps, a bag of nuts with the word 'nuts' picked out on it in sequins, etc. I actually now think this sounds amazing and witty and would like to wear it again. Anyway, there was another girl in the class who was beautiful and extremely cool and went to a different school. She turned up dressed in a very sophisticated 1990 outfit of black trousers, a muted mustard sweater and a black wide-brimmed hat. She looked at my t-shirt with utter contempt and said, 'Haha. *Nuts*.' I felt myself dying inside, profoundly humiliated by this stylish girl's withering comment. I went home and told my mother that I didn't want to dress like a kid anymore. I remember that, at my behest, she very kindly went through all her old clothes and gave me three or four sweaters and t-shirts in mustard, olive and rust colours. I then wore nothing but those three or four tops with black skirts and trousers for about a year. [AvT]

Alex in her 'nuts' t-shirt

Alex recalled going through a grunge phase in her teens, influenced by pop culture and the music she was listening to at the time:

> I remember as a youngish teenager having very strong desires for clothes which signalled an identification with the music I listened to – at the time, grunge and Riot Grrrl. I was obsessed with getting a pair of Doc Martens, which I eventually did. [AvT]

What about university? Both of my daughters had been educated at a single-sex girls' school. They then went on to Oxford, to colleges which had originally been for men only but were now mixed. For Eugénie, who read engineering and computing science at Magdalen, the experience was liberating:

> At university I went through a bit of a *kawaii* phase with wide-legged jeans, big trainers and bubblegum-pink Pokémon t-shirts.
>
> I wouldn't say I was influenced by other students, at least not in terms of their personal style, but I did feel like it was a far less judgemental group than at the high school. Some people turned up in suits, others in ballgowns, others in tracksuit bottoms, and I didn't really hear anybody comment on it. It took me only a few months to ditch most of the clothes I'd worn at school and start playing with unusual shapes and colours. I found my style moving away from attempted sophistication and more towards wit – like putting pink mascara in my hair to match my fingernails. I would say that, in general, people didn't really seem to care and it wasn't a big deal. There was some security guard outside a local bar that used to shout 'Matrix girl!!' at me every time I walked past in my floor-length leather coat, but none of the students ever really expressed an opinion. [EvT]

Alex recalled the move to Oxford (she read history at University College) as heightening her awareness of gender:

> By the time I got to university I had gone past grunge and was dressing really quite smartly. I didn't wear jeans. I wore sharp bootcut trousers, stiletto bitch boots and a lot of leopardskin. Always lots of make-up and eyeliner. I was specifically asserting myself as a disruptive woman in a heavily patriarchal university environment. I went to a college where there were three male students to every female student – four to one in history, which was my subject. But it wasn't just about challenging men – some of those men were brilliant and became lifelong friends. It was about challenging patriarchy. I rejected anything that felt like it recalled soft, self-effacing femininity – floral prints, pastel colours – and consciously embraced a femininity that was hard-edged, challenging and dominant. It was a form of drag: dressing as the woman I wanted to be. [AvT]

The influence of peer groups on clothing style is clear from the foregoing, but it can be permissive or restricting, and peer group pressures operate in conjunction with a range of other factors. Both Alex and Eugénie enjoyed dressing up and playing with identities. For Eugénie, gothic and fantasy worlds were important:

> I don't know why but a gothy, dramatic aesthetic has always appealed to me. I remember watching Tim Burton's films, *Rocky Horror*, *The Addams Family* and so on in my youth and falling in love with the look. Winona Ryder's red dress in *Beetlejuice* blew my mind when I first saw it, aged ten, but it was nothing compared to Winona Ryder's even better red dress in Bram Stoker's *Dracula*, which came along when I was twelve – I had simply never seen anything I loved so much

(I still feel the same way and went to see the dress in person at the V&A when it came to visit a few years ago). Wednesday and Morticia Addams, elegant, witty and intimidating, left me awestruck with excitement and envy of their amazing, fantasy lives. To be honest, I'm still in awe of some of the visuals in these films – Magenta in *Rocky Horror*, Christina Ricci in *Sleepy Hollow*, Miss Argentina in *Beetlejuice*, Mrs Lovett in *Sweeney Todd*. Writing this has made me realise that costume was my gateway into loving and making clothing, as these visuals grabbed me and never let me go, so I started reproducing them, conscious of the fact that I kind of looked like all of these characters at the time. Over the years I've dressed as Wednesday, as Morticia, as Magenta, as Mrs Lovett, and as Xena, Warrior Princess, of course. Xena came about for different reasons – ironically, I'd never seen the TV show and I still haven't (we didn't have satellite!). I don't really know how I'd become aware of her, but I loved the idea of the show as soon as I heard of it. A superbly naff New Zealand fantasy show, looking somehow futuristic and twenty years out of date simultaneously, which had pissed off conservatives by toying with possible bisexuality of the two lead characters, thus immediately guaranteeing massive 'queer icon' status, all while looking like the She-Ra figures of my youth... well, I was sold. I'd also started becoming increasingly eager to make costumes, and I didn't know how to sew, so I figured armour was a good place to start. I didn't know anybody else who was making elaborate costumes, or who was interested in doing so, so I felt quite isolated and quite strange for wanting to. A couple of years later, the internet would introduce me to the world of cosplay, and I would come to realise I was far from alone. [EvT]

CHAPTER FIFTEEN

Leaving university and starting work brought both new opportunities and new constraints. I asked my daughters whether they had ever read or been influenced by fashion magazines. Eugénie stated categorically that she hadn't:

> I've never read fashion magazines. My style influences were characters from film and TV, with the exception of Jean Paul Gaultier, who is the only figure in the fashion industry I've ever adored. [EvT]

Alex's reply was very different:

> I obsessively read fashion magazines for a while – I even did work experience at *Vogue*, and then stayed on after my three weeks of work experience to cover for the assistant to the deputy editor. It was at the end of the 1990s, in the wake of designers like Jean Paul Gaultier, John Galliano and Alexander McQueen, who had turned fashion into a form of art. I really believed that it was an art at that time. Working at *Vogue* briefly was the beginning of a process of disillusionment. I was disappointed that relatively few of the editorial discussions I heard revealed any real interest in ideas. It was mostly just about which brands were advertising, and who was in the team's in-crowd, and therefore what should go in the magazine from a commercial and socially elitist point of view. I had spent quite a lot of energy defending my love of fashion from implications that it was superficial, snobby and all about capitalism. Anyway, when I got to *Vogue*, I found out very quickly that at that level it really was superficial, snobby and all about capitalism. I'm very glad I discovered that aged twenty: I ditched all notions of working in that industry and my own interest in clothes shifted far more to forms of street style

and anti-fashion. I mostly shopped in super discounted sales outlets and charity shops for ages after that. [AvT]

As adult women working in the creative industries both my daughters have enjoyed considerable freedom in what they can wear: Alex, as a writer, has often found herself resorting to comfort clothes unless 'on show' in some way, and unsurprisingly, during the Covid years this tendency was accentuated:

> When I'm writing I wear sweatpants and t-shirts. Comfort is the only consideration. If I have to go to an in-person meeting, I will put on 'real' clothes, with the style depending on what sort of meeting it is and therefore how smart I need to look. I usually dress smartly when I appear on TV or give public talks, quite often in a dress. I almost feel it's respectful to the audience to appear well presented.
>
> [During lockdown] I effectively wore pyjamas for two years. I still wear 'lockdown clothes' most of the time at home. [AvT]

Eugénie considered that work had impacted on her style of dress rather less than might be imagined from her senior management status because the company employs creative types:

> I suppose I'm technically a manager, which might be associated with conservative dress, but the only people I've ever seen sporting 'smart' dress in the office are visitors from other parts of the world. Jeans are fine, but we're in the entertainment world, so more creativity is definitely appreciated and valued. I'm sure one of the reasons I get invited to so many speaking engagements is because I'm memorable, and that includes the way I present myself. So

> I guess I'm encouraged to dress as casual or as fancy as I like. The exception is on-site work, of course, when I'm in waterproofs and safety boots. [EvT]

Eugénie was clear that the biggest change in what she wears had come about when she fulfilled a longstanding ambition to start sewing, and making her own clothes:

> I still felt quite studenty for a good few years after leaving university, in the sense that I didn't have disposable income or particularly expensive desires. I'd tried wandering over to Selfridges to see if it excited me, but it didn't, really. Not my style. As I mentioned above, I sort of vaguely drifted in and out of phases through my twenties, but I would say the next significant change was when I started sewing in 2013, some ten years ago now. Sewing changed my feelings towards clothes. Instead of worrying about whether I looked sexy/stylish/'well cut', I just started enjoying the process of combining my favourite colours, prints and shapes. I find myself not hugely caring how they look when they're on – I'm proud of the creativity and enjoy the sense of uniqueness. [EvT]

With her work in the film industry, and later, on theme park rides, my younger daughter has attended a number of international award ceremonies over the last few years, and these have required serious thought about what to wear:

> I've been to three awards ceremonies in the last decade – the Oscars, the Baftas and the VES (Visual Effects Society) awards. At the Oscars, I wore a new Vivienne Westwood dress. At the Baftas, I wore vintage. At the VES awards, I made my own dress. With hindsight, I liked the one I made the best, because it was unique, and totally my sense of humour. The

Eugénie in her skull dress

vintage was second best – it was so dramatic. The Westwood was cool but, I guess, my least favourite – and that realisation was quite significant for me, because it was easily the most expensive. I can afford expensive clothes, now, but I don't buy them at all. They're just not as interesting to me as making or repurposing stuff. [EvT]

The dress Eugénie made for the VES awards ceremony was full length; a dark teal in colour, with tumbling, appliquéd skulls in silver lamé. When planning to go to the Scientific and Technical Oscars ceremony in LA, early in 2023, she decided to wear a dress that she had fashioned out of a duvet cover.

Both Alex and Eugénie rejected any idea that they might be thinking about men or women's separate reactions when deciding on how to dress. Alex responded firmly:

> I don't think I differentiate. I think a lot about the context of patriarchy – see my thoughts on university dressing above – but I wouldn't simplify that into a men versus women divide. In my experience, there are such huge ranges of reactions within the categories 'men' and 'women' (informed by all sorts of factors such as their races, sexualities, religions, etc.) that it doesn't make sense to split them into those two camps. [AvT]

Similarly, Eugénie retorted that:

> I don't object to your question, but, I have to say, I've never gender-divided this thought. I do sometimes ask myself how people see my clothes. I don't mind if people don't notice my clothes, but I do hope they do, only because I hope it brings them joy. [EvT]

Even so, both women were keenly aware of how they were perceived for dressing the way they did. Alex had no doubt that politics as distinct from gender came into this:

> In terms of reactions to how I present myself, I'd say, for instance, that the divide between conservatives and progressives is far more significant. I usually have blue hair and this sometimes provokes fury online from very conservative men and women alike. One American woman argued with me for ages online about why it was fine for her to dye her hair blonde but, in her opinion, it was appalling and unnatural for me to dye my hair blue. It's funny how personally some people take it when you present yourself in a way that, in their opinion, transgresses acceptable social norms. I was once ridiculed online by a self-identified Nazi – someone whose bio was a 1933 quote from Hitler about a Jewish conspiracy, with a banner picture from a Nuremberg Rally – for having blue hair, so immediately I went and dyed it even bluer. Political extremists are real and frightening, but these petty reactions just amuse me: why on earth would I be concerned about what some unknown person halfway across the world thinks of my look? If I saw them, perhaps I wouldn't care for how they dressed either – but, really, it's none of my business, and I doubt I could get worked up about it. [AvT]

Alex found different cultural reactions to her appearance equally intriguing: on a visit to India she had worn an embroidered kurta over trousers. Travelling from India to Cuba, she had wanted to wear the same clothes:

> I find long, loose cotton garments perfect for the tropical sun, because my skin burns so easily. But wearing long sleeves and trousers in Havana makes you stand out a mile: the cultural norm there is extremely casual clothing and most people were in crop tops and tiny shorts. I was there with a friend from Latin America, and she kept laughing at me and telling me to take more clothes off because I looked like a complete weirdo and the locals thought there was something terribly wrong with me. [AvT]

Eugénie told me that in choosing clothes, she likes to be noticed, and she hopes that her appearance will give pleasure and make people smile. She volunteered two anecdotes about this. The first concerned an experience when she had been working on the film *Interstellar*, during the shoot:

> I was stationed in the London office, doing video calls to Iceland every day. One of the members of the location crew, senior to me, called in. 'Is Eugénie there yet?' I heard him say, while I headed over to the camera from my desk. 'What's she wearing?'
>
> I was about to respond pretty negatively. It's creepy for an older guy to get on the phone and ask what a young woman is wearing, and totally irrelevant to our work. But, before I could respond, he continued. 'We all look forward to seeing her every day,' he explained. 'She's like a joyful explosion of colour in our cold, drab, North Face world.'
>
> As you can no doubt imagine, my negativity completely evaporated. It's really quite lovely to think of my outfit

bringing joy to people, and I guess the real reason for wearing fun outfits is to make people smile.

Eugénie's second story centred around the style of another person:

I was at SIGGRAPH, a vast computer graphics conference in Los Angeles, and I was moaning to a co-worker about the lack of diversity. 'My god,' I whined. 'Look at this. Hundreds... thousands... of men in their thirties in faded black software t-shirts. Beards. Messy hair. Everybody's bloody identical.'
My friend shrugged. 'Well, not her,' he said, pointing.
I spun around to see a large space on the convention centre floor peppered with tables and chairs, packed with armies of tech dudes on laptops. Among them, also working away at her computer, was a tiny lady, maybe middle-aged, sporting a neon pink and lime green Victorian-style crinoline dress. Her cat's-eye glasses were neon pink. Her lace-covered parasol, inexplicably shielding her from the fluorescent lights of the convention centre, was lime green and trimmed with lace. She wore lace gloves and high heels. My first thought was that she must be some kind of actor, there to advertise a product or for photo opportunities, but no – she was just attending the conference like that. My second thought was a flush of joy and pride as I realised this was a friend of mine – Dara [Dara McGarry], an old co-worker whom I'd always adored, for her infectiously joyful spirit as well as her love of costume and colour. My third thought was simply that this one act, turning up to a techbro conference in this completely ridiculous outfit, was the coolest thing I had ever seen in my life. She barely even seemed to be aware that she'd done it. She'd just put it on. Nobody was laughing. And, yet, ten years later, I still remember it, and I still think it's the coolest thing I've ever seen anybody do. [EvT]

What do I learn from all this? Quite a lot. My daughters' childhood experiences of clothes, like my own, tended to be sensuous; memories crystallising through colour, texture and feel. Later, through schooling, peer group influence and pressures come to bear, often bringing a sense of insecurity and shame. Young teenagers need to establish selves separate from their parents, to feel at ease in different environments, and to belong. Young people privileged to go to university can play with their appearance, it is part of trying to find out who one is, to establish an identity. University can liberate, but it also introduces new reference groups capable of shaming or applauding personal style. The pressures of the workplace have a similar effect, but here, social class and the character of the industry matter. Creative industries allow more license than other kinds of corporate employment, and working at home can do away with expectations about smartness in dress.

Have my daughters been less troubled about the way they dress than I have been? Alex confessed that she had felt anxiety about clothes at times in her life when she had put on weight and felt less than happy with her body; 'When you aren't happy with your body, dressing stops being a pleasure and starts being an exercise in "what can I wear that minimises how unacceptable I look?"' she observed. At such times desire might turn away from clothes and one might find oneself thinking about accessories or handbags:

> When I was very slim, I didn't really understand why other women were preoccupied with handbags, shoes and jewellery: now I suspect it is at least partly because your shape or size are irrelevant to the enjoyment of these things. They give me that endorphin hit of pleasure and sense of luxury that clothes once did. I don't have the budget for fine jewels or high-end designer bags (a Chanel classic handbag is over £7,000 now, for heaven's sake!) – and in any case I am

far too likely to lose or damage anything really expensive. But I do love unusual handmade things and independent designers. My favourite handbag was bought in Lebanon from an incredible shop called Sarah's Bag. The company trains underprivileged women, mostly prisoners and ex-prisoners, in artisanal beading techniques. The resulting bags are a delight: designs like Beirut graffiti, Xanax boxes and tattoo-style hearts picked out in the most sumptuous beading. There are definitely echoes here of that M&S Nuts t-shirt that I was shamed for as a teenager. It turns out I still love it. [AvT]

Alex also confessed to environmental concerns and aspired to buying less in recent years, and aiming to recycle. Eugénie now dyes and prints fabrics, and makes almost all her own clothes. Both of my daughters have opted for starkly dramatic tattoos, a form of adornment quite separate from the categories of jewellery or make-up discussed earlier in this book. When I asked whether they considered themselves to have a consistent style, both women replied decisively in the negative. 'Not at all,' was Alex's response. 'God, no,' replied her sister. This intrigued me, since I think, deep down, I *do* upbraid myself for inconsistency in style and dress: I sometimes think that I should have worked things out, have more integrity by now. Asked to comment on their mother's attitudes to clothes, both daughters were kind. Eugénie conceded that there may have been social and historical reasons for my unease over the years:

> Sometimes I think back to how hard it must have been for you to be taken seriously as an academic when you started out… and you were young, glamorous and covered in eyeliner. [EvT]

On the other hand, she thought many of my anxieties had a more personal/psychological root. Alex thought it paradoxical that I should talk about 'agonising' over clothes when it was clear to her that I *enjoyed* them so much:

> I suppose maybe there is a level of guilt about spending money or enjoying things that don't seem intellectually sophisticated. I find this a bit puritanical. Though I do think most of us should probably consume less from an environmental point of view – but consuming less might well entail buying fewer things of better quality, so it's not necessarily an act of self-denial. [AvT]

'What is the cause of your agony?' asked Alex. Ah! Writing this book has been an attempt, in part, to unravel, to trace back some of those pulled threads.

SIXTEEN

Dress and Desire

I OFTEN FIND MYSELF PONDERING Miuccia Prada's remark, quoted at the beginning of this book, to the effect that sometimes she found herself wondering whether the obsession with fashion was 'just about the desperation of being sexy'. Interviewed for a profile in the *New York Times* in 2004, she observed that her young assistants tended to come to work wearing 'amazing things. Very provocative,' but that they were always alone. 'And I tell them that the more they dress for sex, the less sex they will have. It is so basic, but they don't seem to understand me.'

It isn't hard to find evidence of the ways in which women desperately seeking partners, or finding themselves in unsatisfactory love affairs, turn to buying clothes. As discussed in Chapter 1, when Rebecca West was marooned as a single mother on the Essex coast, and pining for the presence of the married H.G. Wells, she found her stress manifested in nervous illness and skin eruptions. She sought solace in impulse buying, including extravagant 'silk evening knickers' and other luxuries from expensive shops. Nobel-prize winning French author Annie Ernaux has published two books documenting her obsessive and painful affair in mid-life with a younger married man. Both comment on the way in which sexual obsession fed into an obsession with clothes. In *Getting Lost*, a less filtered and constructed account of her daily experience than *Simple Passion*, Ernaux writes of 'the constant interplay between love and the desire for clothes, insatiable, though I suspect futile with regard to desire in general'. She compares her experience in this respect with that during an earlier affair, 'when I continually bought skirts, jumpers, dresses, etc. never looking at the price – spending as if there were no tomorrow'. In both texts Ernaux confesses to spending much of her time, when alone, daydreaming about clothes and jewellery, trying them on in front of a mirror, striving for perfection – even though her encounters with her lover were of short duration, and these clothes would be glimpsed only briefly before they were torn off and consigned to a heap on the floor. Both Rebecca West's and Ernaux's accounts resonate with the idea of clothes reflecting 'the desperation of being sexy'.

Women can invest colossally in trying to make themselves attractive to potential lovers. There's a brilliantly detailed account in Viv Albertine's memoir, *To Throw Away Unopened* (2018). She describes a brief trip to a hotel in Rye with a male companion (hardly lover, but she hoped for some potential there). The trip required serious planning and packing. Appointments with hairdresser and beautician. Threading, plucking, pedicure. An overnight bag laden with carefully selected clothing, underwear, footwear choices and cosmetics. Viv – who had styled herself as a rebel when a young guitarist in the punk band, The Slits, details all this meticulous preparation with wry humour and a certain amount of feminist indignation: 'Not one man I know, have known, or have dated in the last forty-five years has ever, or would ever, put the amount of effort into himself that I put into that date – just to feel comfortable.' The date wasn't a success. She decided not to repeat the experience: she just 'couldn't be arsed' to put the effort in for so little reward.

An interesting aspect of this account is that Albertine

emphasises that whilst aiming to look attractive, she had judged it inadvisable to look *too* sexy in case her companion felt daunted. She had bought a new designer bra for the occasion, underwired, in black mesh – with characteristic self-deprecating humour she tells us that it squashed her nipples and made her breasts look 'like two milky jellyfish trawled up from Dungeness beach'. She decided against wearing matching knickers in case her date jumped to the conclusion that she was expecting a raunchy performance from him in bed. Opting for plain black pants from Gap suggested lower and more realisable aspirations – it was an attempt to boost confidence on both sides. As it turned out, Viv tells us that she kept an old, worn-out grey t-shirt on in bed, with the hotel's white waffle bathrobe on top. Nuanced considerations about facilitating seduction proved a waste of time: she never wore the bra again and eventually threw it away.

What do we mean by describing clothing as 'sexy', 'seductive' or 'provocative'? Looking up 'sexy clothing' on the internet yields a number of entries so large – around 1,810,000,000, last time I tried it – that it is difficult to express verbally. (I think this translates as one billion eight hundred and ten million entries.) The results in terms of images are predictable. Latex plunge skater outfits, dominatrix gear, lots of black lace and 'bodycon'. And yes – those underwired, push-up, black or red mesh bras. The term 'provocative' is deeply troubling, of course. In societies characterised by sexual inequality (which is most places, although to differing extents), it has long been associated with blaming women. In Christianity, Adam blames Eve for tempting him with the apple. Eve is associated with serpentine wiles; it was all *her* fault.

Feminism can have little truck with this. The idea of women 'inviting' rape through wearing sexy clothing is indefensible. In 2011, a Canadian security officer's suggestion at York University, Toronto, to the effect that if women wanted to avoid rape they shouldn't dress like 'sluts', led to rallies and protest marches which quickly spread around the globe. The concept of 'provocative' clothing all too easily leads to victim blaming. But it has proved hard to shift prejudice on this score. In a 2022 case in Kerala, for instance, a judge dismissed a sexual assault case against a seventy-four-year-old man on the grounds of the victim having been dressed 'provocatively'. There was an immediate outcry, and a couple of months later the High Court in Kerala criticised these remarks, noting that 'a victim's attire could not be construed as legal ground to absolve an accused from the charge of outraging the modesty of a woman'.

Men's clothes are very rarely described as 'provocative'. Nor do we hear much about masculine modesty. In his recent study of the Bloomsbury artistic circle and their attitudes to clothes, fashion writer Charlie Porter unpicks the sartorial habits of novelist E.M. Forster in the 1900s. Forster's unease about his homosexuality was reflected in understatement and reserve, buttoned-up suits and an exaggerated adherence to conventional tailoring. This may have been partly to reassure himself, partly self-defence and an attempt to deflect criticism. Gay men might well have been pilloried or laughed at for any flamboyance in dress, but the tone of such criticism was usually quite different from that levelled at those perceived as wicked or 'scarlet' women. As many have observed, the idea of women being shamed and censored for 'provocative clothing' sustains deeply problematic attitudes about agency, the legitimacy of desire and women's responsibility for male sexual behaviour.

These terms — 'modesty', 'provocative', even 'sexy' — are of course loose and hard to pin down. They depend on context, intentions and subjective or cultural interpretations. In Afghanistan under Taliban rule, women have to cover themselves completely: femaleness, presumably, is in itself immodest, amounting to a provocation. In Iran a woman can be bullied by the morality police for not wearing a hijab – the tragedy of Mahsa Amini, who many are convinced was beaten to death by those who objected to her wearing her headscarf 'improperly', slipping back on her head, fired international outrage. There can be little agreement over what constitutes a 'provocative' appearance when mere bare-headedness can be seen in this light. And we shouldn't forget that sexuality, repressed, can bubble up in polymorphous and perverse forms. Schoolgirl uniforms were designed for modesty, but soon became invested with eroticism and fetishised. Nuns' habits and nurses' uniforms carry similar potential. It is worth thinking back to the Victorian obsession with corsets and tight lacing: some have construed this as indicative of female objectification, oppression and a form of fetishism. But many contemporaries – women as well as men – saw the corset as representing a kind of decent containment or modesty (as in 'straitlaced'). To reject 'stays' and to free or flaunt the natural body was sometimes seen as the hallmark of the hoyden.

Dress and desire are nevertheless closely linked, however much we problematise definitions and stereotypes. In Western culture, little girls grow up amidst a barrage of messages about beautiful dresses, frocks and gowns that will make *them* beautiful. Clothes that will turn ugly ducklings into swans; Cinderellas into fairy princesses. The belief that looking beautiful will make a handsome prince love you is enshrined at the heart of romance. Girls fantasise about dresses: a ball dress, a prom dress, a wedding dress. A red dress, carrying messages about boldness and sophisticated sensuality. A white dress, with pink rosebuds, misty with romance. Like so many girls and women who were and are avid readers, from an early age I devoured descriptions of clothes in literature. These ignited desires to find a style that would inspire, flatter and perfect. Literature, to me, was richer as a source for these imaginings than cinema or fashion magazines. Though all of these contributed to fantasies of what to wear.

I've been seriously 'in love' some five times during the course of my life, and looking back, it was these involvements, whether troubled or particularly happy, that led me to buy too many clothes. When I met my first serious boyfriend, at university, I made many outfits, trying to look trendy and desirable. Later, when I became involved with the man I married, I delighted in buying fashionable stuff from boutiques, in bright colours. What I bought reflected happiness and a lack of sophistication at that time. I was uncertain about personal style, somewhere between career woman academic and dollybird. It makes me cringe a bit now. As I got older, I turned to black. It felt safe. A later love affair had me buying lots of underwear, often impractical, in cream silk and satin. It was a point in my life when I rediscovered – or maybe started to learn about – sexuality. Driven by powerful desire and longing, I tried desperately not to let these derail the rest of my life; my roles as mother, teacher, scholarly researcher. But I remember clothes that were shrill with body awareness: stretchy burgundy velvet, a clingy sweater dress in raspberry pink fluffy angora. There was a red woollen sweater dress which required much clenching of stomach muscles. I tried too hard at that stage, I find myself reflecting, ruefully. I hope now to have arrived at a greater self-awareness. Although I still buy too many clothes.

Miuccia Prada has been described as 'a fashion intellectual': she is sharply intelligent as well as highly successful in her work as a cutting-edge designer. When she spoke of 'the desperation of being sexy' and suggested that too much attention to sexiness and perfection in one's presentation of self could be counter-productive in terms of attracting others, she meant more than just the kind of view expressed by the poet Ovid, when he observed that 'Too rich a dress may sometimes check desire.' An obsessive concern with the way one looks can certainly signal untouchability, a kind of brittle self-absorption. But more than this, Prada has effectively revolutionised what we may think of as 'sexy'. The house is often credited with making ugliness sexy. Prada outfits play on the theme of contradictions, liminality, the knife-edge borderline between frumpiness and an exquisite chic. Fashion writer Daniel Rodgers drew attention to the way in which Prada brought wrinkled socks and big knickers into high fashion. Miuccia Prada, he declared, 'knows that true eroticism is transgressive'.

To dress to look desirable, then, is never straightforward. It is easy to get it wrong. But dressing to look desirable, and dressing for the sake of one's own ease and pleasure, aren't after all poles apart. Sensuous fabrics, soft shoes, creamy cosmetics: all these can offer comfort as well as pleasure. In 1917, a young Rebecca West wrote to her friend Sylvia Lynd, confessing that she had used the cheque representing the earnings from her first novel to buy an expensive hat: the *most* expensive hat that she had ever bought in her life. The hat was to cheer herself up, unsettled as she was by news of military events in Italy: 'the hat was a direct consequence of the Italian disaster. All these war horrors, instead of making me ascetic, make me turn furiously to sensuous delights.' At such times, she thought there was an impulse to reassure oneself that life was worth living, through the enjoyment of simple pleasures. During air raids, she observed, 'I don't pray or speculate on the world state, but drench myself in scent and eat chocolates.' Most of us will know exactly what she meant.

SEVENTEEN

History through Clothes

ANGELA CARTER'S LAST NOVEL, *Wise Children* (1991), is an exuberant celebration of life as performance. It celebrates femininity and the love of dressing up, even in old age. Well into their seventies, twin sisters Dora and Nora Chance flaunt themselves in silver fox-fur trench coats and tights with silver stars on them. They delight in painting their faces and gamely glam up, wryly aware – but not too bothered by – warnings that cosmetics risk giving women over a certain age the look of female impersonators. It is a joy to dress up, to dance and sing, and joy affirms human resilience in the knowledge of death, which counts for a great deal.

Dressing up was for Carter always a subject of fascination, and her novels abound in references to clothes. There is a poignant scene in *Wise Children* where Dora and Nora go through their dead grandmother's wardrobe. It proved a potent trip down Memory Lane. They discovered piles of lingerie, 'silk, satin, lace, eau-de-nil, blush rose, flesh, black and red ribbons, straight up and down things from the twenties, slithering things from the thirties, curvy things from the forties, waspies, merry widows, uplift bras'. At the bottom of the pile they were moved to discover the navy blue bloomers they had worn as young girls at a dancing class, their grandma (who had brought the girls up) having kept these for sentimental reasons. The wardrobe was full of frocks, some ('bias cut silk jersey, beaded sheaths that weighed a ton') stored in plastic bags; others ('the big net skirts, the taffeta crinolines') covered in sheets. The girls piled the contents of the wardrobe on the bed and eyed them meditatively. Should they donate the stuff to the V&A? 'Half a century of evening wear,' mused Nora. 'A history of the world in party frocks.'

Many women have toyed with the idea of telling the story of their lives through clothing. Writer Linda Grant prefaced her book *The Thoughtful Dresser* by asserting that she could write her autobiography in terms of analysing her clothes from birth to the present. She discovered that when she tried to look back on her life, and to understand her earlier selves, she regularly found herself thinking about what she had worn. 'Clothes are a lifelong journey into acquiring an identity,' she writes. 'When you start to dress yourself, you are beginning your own future, the subtle, everyday construction of who you are through what you wear.'

Grant's book is not primarily an autobiography, although there are many sections of personal insight and self-reflection within its pages. Perhaps more autobiographical, though with a very light touch, is Ilene Beckerman's *Love, Loss and What I Wore* (2005). Beckerman's book muses on the clothes she has worn since childhood, which she illustrates with simple line drawings. Fragmentary memories are hooked on to particular outfits, like commentary in a photo album. She remembers, for instance, the dress she wore (a coral wool jersey in an A-line with boat neck and princess styling) when she first planned to 'go all the way' with her boyfriend George, though she didn't, because her plan was foiled by 'car trouble'. Beckerman remembers the dress she wore as a bridesmaid, and the black turtleneck jersey and 'gray quilted circle skirt' with 'a wide leather belt from Greenwich village' that she wore as a fashionable teenager. Her wedding dress, when as a twenty-year-old she married her thirty-seven-year-old sociology professor from university, was a princess-style number in pink satin. The marriage didn't last. A little later Beckerman records that, with her husband Harry's encouragement, she had bought an iridescent brocaded Chinese-style dinner dress for a dinner party in Massachusetts. She had loved the dress and felt good about the way it had showed off her arms. But at midnight she had come across Harry kissing another woman, and we must suppose that that was the beginning of the end. The next entry in the book describes a yellow ochre wool dress which she borrowed from a flatmate in New York. Beckerman's book takes us through her life, outfits used as stepping-stones, standing for life events: her second marriage, which also failed, the death of a baby son. We learn a little about her personal style, influenced by Audrey Hepburn and Rita Hayworth; where she shopped (Bloomingdales, Bonwit Teller, Neiman Marcus); her guilt about misguided purchases, shared with her therapist. We are treated to glimpses of both personal and fashion history through the clothes.

More intimately personal, if still not exactly an autobiography, is Claire Wilcox's haunting collection of reflections, *Patch Work; A Life Among Clothes*. Wilcox interweaves fragments of memory with her expertise as a senior curator of costume at the V&A. The poignant associations of objects and surfaces remembered and treasured since childhood; the sensuousness of touch, of knowing something through the fingertips; the softness of linen fibres; the brightness of buttons, all spark meditations on love and loss. The result is poetic and often mesmerising. Wilcox writes with both intimacy and professionalism, which don't always go together. Curators of costume collections are often asked whether they are tempted to try on the clothes they conserve. When asked in public, their professionalism usually prevails: they demur, say they wouldn't dream of it. But Wilcox confesses that she did once dream of trying on an ermine coat, feeling 'the cool fur brush against' her cheek; 'It would have been so simple to put my arms into its folds and feel its extravagant cruelty. I think of it still, imagine its weight, the sly sensuality of satin and fur and skin.' She restrained herself, there was work to do. The episode has resonance with recent issues. In the spring of 2022, the media erupted with controversy when American socialite Kim Kardashian levered herself into the legendary dress worn by Marilyn Monroe to serenade President J.F. Kennedy on his forty-fifth birthday, straining the flesh-coloured soufflé silk embellished with tiny crystal beads. Conservationists were understandably horrified.

The Monroe dress episode fitly illustrates the ways in which the history of dress is bound up with the history of desire. Wilcox's knowledge of the history of dress through the senses, through touch and feelings as well as through colour and line, amplifies this. The feelings aren't easy to pin down, but we learn about the faded apron evoking the soft, floury arms of her Welsh grandmother making apple pie; 'the marvellous tonic to the senses' offered by a glimpse of the V&A's collection of Fortuny Delphos gowns, their lustrous silken pleats 'coiled into fat rolls' in a mahogany drawer. The colours of these alone astonish: 'crushed marigold, Tiepolo pink, silver-grey, teal, salmon, pale blue, ivory and black. The most expensive are dusted with gold; stencilled with Greek key patterns and medieval fleur-de-lys.' Wilcox notes that opening the drawer to reveal such riches to visitors regularly elicits a potent but complex emotional reaction, expressed through 'sighs of desire and regret'.

Reviewing C. Willett Cunningham's book, *English Women's Clothing in the Nineteenth Century*, when it was first published in 1937, novelist Elizabeth Bowen emphasised that 'Dress has never been at all a straightforward business: so much subterranean interest and complex feeling attaches to it.' It was, she insisted, a dangerous topic, with 'a flowery head but deep roots in the passions'. Discussions of the subject often proved a minefield: talking about 'love, food, politics, art or money' was much safer. Just *why*, Linda Grant pondered some decades later, did she feel so *driven* to go out one morning to buy a pair of extremely expensive and impractical, 'indeed impossible', high-heeled shoes? What was her unconscious mind trying to tell her? Many will recognise the impulse, even whilst not fully understanding. Paul Gallico's story mentioned in an earlier chapter, *Flowers for Mrs Harris* (recently turned into the film *Mrs Harris Goes to Paris* starring Lesley Manville and Isabelle Huppert), focused on a widowed charwoman with a desperate desire to possess a Dior dress.

There can be no doubt that feelings, fantasies and desires around clothing provide historians of the emotions with a rich source of material, albeit that references to such in diaries and autobiographies can be fragmentary, laborious to collate and not easy — indeed rarely straightforward — to interpret. Then there is the question of moving from the personal to the social: how far can we generalise from particular cases? What kind of story could we tell (returning to Nora Chance's vision in Angela Carter's novel)? Should we try to 'write a history of the world in party frocks'?

It is worth remembering that most social history shares the challenge of relating individual experience to that of the wider social context: in respect of the history of dress this challenge is particularly pertinent because clothing itself bridges the separation between the personal and the social. The ways in which this is manifest will vary; choices, behaviour and habits will be filtered through social position and individual psychology. Some people dress for respectability, to conform. Others – such as the lady mentioned earlier in this book, who scandalised her husband's golf club in décolleté fuchsia Courtelle – were out to challenge conventions or even to court trouble.

There aren't any simple patterns. Social and costume historians may – and do – put forward reasonably convincing generalisations about the relationship of clothing to social change. These observations might sometimes seem obvious: that women keen to embrace the freedoms offered by the bicycle sometimes opted for knickerbockers or 'Rational Dress', for instance, or that bathing costumes, short skirts and 'beach pyjamas' came into fashion with the enthusiasm for sunbathing and cruise ships in the 1920s and 1930s. But equally, movements in fashion, as distinct from individual preferences, can appear to run counter to, rather than to reflect, social trends. If liberated 'New Women' in the 1890s wore simplified clothes to allow more freedom of movement, they also espoused heavy draped skirts, corsets and bustles. It might be thought that suffrage campaigners in the 1900s would have needed to feel agile, joining in street processions and skirmishes; nevertheless they often chose to wear 'hobble skirts' and massive, flamboyant hats. And in the 1950s, in spite of some feminist cavilling about the voluminous skirts and corseted waists of the New Look,' many career-minded women openly delighted in the new, unashamedly feminine lines. Linda Grant suggested that the clothes of the 1960s made possible new social and sexual freedoms. 'It's impossible to imagine the woman's movement dressed in the New Look', she contended. But historians no longer insist on the 1950s as a time when feminism was decisively backfooted. Rather, the decade is represented as a time rife with contradictions; the potential for social change incubating or bubbling away beneath the surface.

Dress can't be held simply to reflect nor to precipitate social change: the relation between the two continues to perplex. Elizabeth Bowen emphasised the psychological complexity inherent in choosing clothes: writing in the 1930s she judged that those rich enough to rely on *couture* were paying a price for safety, whereas those of moderate income were 'thrown back among… anxieties… fixations… will-o'-the-wispish personal fantasies'. They were likely to go in for uneasy, tentative dressing, and much more likely to be tricked by false views of themselves. The English middle class, she opined, was the stronghold of 'compromise dressing'. This resonates with historian Catherine Horwood's work on fashion and social class in the 1920s and 1930s. In her book, *Keeping Up Appearances* (2005), Horwood emphasised the myriad ways in which dress codes signalled respectability as a governing principle of – and source of anxiety in – middle-class life between the wars.

Bowen had little to say in her essay about the more economically constrained masses. Her contemporaries were often much more vocal. Many were made uneasy by the influence of Hollywood cinema on the aspirations and appearance of working-class girls. Writers J.B. Priestley and Thomas Burke both remarked on how factory girls had discarded shawls and clogs and were using cosmetics and fashionable clothes 'to look like actresses'. George Orwell similarly picked up on developments in mass-market fashion since the 1914–18 war, which, he observed, had allowed working-class girls to indulge in daydreams of themselves as Greta Garbo. Dress, in these cases, was increasingly seen to have become aspirational, signifying the desire for glamour, a tool in aspirations for social mobility rather than a fittingly modest expression of respectability and social position.

Decisions about appearance were likely to be constrained by means and filtered through personal values and psychology. Clothes might reflect desire and often embodied dreams. But the choice of clothing, like fashion itself, can reflect a deep ambivalence. Fashion historian Elizabeth Wilson recognised this ambivalence in her now classic study of fashion and modernity, *Adorned in Dreams* (1985). Fashion, she concluded, like modernity, often acts as a vehicle for contradictory and irreconcilable desires. For 'when we dress, we wear inscribed on our bodies the often obscure relationship of art, personal psychology and the social order'. Choosing what to wear can be troubling, particularly in times of social change. This offers a clue to understanding why so many women in modern Britain have found fashion, and clothing choices, perplexing. Sometimes, different ideas, values and identities have literally been fought out on the body. It may not be possible to write a straightforward 'history of the world in party frocks', but social and cultural historians nevertheless mine a rich seam in the history of clothing.

EIGHTEEN

Sorting, Clearing, Letting Go

THE VERB 'TO DECLUTTER' entered the *Oxford English Dictionary* in 2015, although the *OED* entry indicates an early use of the term in the pages of *Vogue* in 1950. Books and TV programmes about decluttering and tidying up have abounded over the last twenty years or so. Marie Kondo's *The Life-Changing Magic of Tidying Up* (2014) and Margareta Magnusson's *The Gentle Art of Swedish Death Cleaning; How to Free Yourself and Your Family from A Lifetime of Clutter* (2017) were both *New York Times* bestsellers. People living in bedsits and small city flats have to be economical about space and can't afford to hoard possessions. Advisors sing the praises of 'capsule wardrobes' and rented storage units. Older people enjoying the luxury of spacious homes consider downsizing, worrying about leaving relatives with the problem of clearing out possessions and paperwork accumulated through decades: what will happen to all this stuff when they die?

We're assured that the Swedish concept of a 'death clean' (*döstädning*) can be liberating rather than a gloomfest, that tidying up the Marie Kondo way (the 'KonMari' method) can bring joy. Not everyone will be convinced.

Queen Victoria was said to be an inveterate hoarder. Lytton Strachey's biography elaborates on her desire to stop time in its tracks. This was most obvious after the death of her beloved

Albert; for decades afterwards, she ordered his room to be serviced and arranged, just as if he still lived. Hot water was to be delivered daily, his clothes pressed and laid out ready for wearing. Victoria kept everything: clothes (her own, since childhood, her mother's), mementoes, papers. According to Strachey, 'she would not lose one memory or one pin. She gave orders that nothing should be thrown away – and nothing was'… 'There, in drawer after drawer, in wardrobe after wardrobe, reposed the dresses of seventy years. But not only the dresses – the furs and the mantles and the subsidiary frills and the muffs and the parasols and the bonnets – all were ranged in chronological order, dated and complete.' Victoria also had the rooms of her homes photographed, further storing memories. She kept all her children's baby teeth, in a highly intricate gilt-metal casket. Those who have visited her summer home at Osborne on the Isle of Wight may have encountered the extraordinary collection of casts of her infant children's limbs, chubby little arms resting on plump crimson velvet cushions. Hoarding and collecting was a defence against loss; Victoria's lists and inventories of belongings proliferated as she aged.

Saga Magazine, aimed in Britain at the over-fifties, published a short piece on clothes in September 2022, written by Rachel Carlyle under the strapline 'Your Wardrobe Secrets'. This claimed that in a poll of 1,700 readers, 73% admitted to keeping clothes that they thought they wouldn't ever wear again. Six in ten of *Saga*'s respondents admitted that they no longer wore at least half of their clothes, and almost half of them confessed to having items which they hadn't ever worn. 'It seems that Marie Kondo and the army of other TV declutterers would have their work cut out with *Saga* customers,' suggested Carlyle. Fashion psychologist Carolyn Mair is quoted as having concluded that 'most people can't stomach mass clear-outs'. There might be many reasons for crammed wardrobes: we may keep things for sentimental reasons, or buy or hold on to clothes that no longer fit us in the hope that we may lose weight one day.

Writer Linda Grant, moving into a smaller flat, realised that she had too many books. They were piled up everywhere, overflowing shelves, accumulating dust. She decided to cull them. She admits that she found the whole process traumatising. In an article published in the *Guardian*, entitled 'I Murdered my Library', she confessed that without her books, everything felt abnormal, wrong: 'the whole business of this move has made me massively insecure, blind-sided everywhere'. For many of us, books are a form of identity, a catalogue of our thinking over the years. As an ageing academic I amassed a huge collection of books, many of them rare historical texts to do with women's lives and the history of feminism. I also inherited my husband's enormous library of books on economic history and mountaineering. Our house couldn't accommodate all of these, the majority of which had been kept in our offices at the university. In addition, for many years I had rented a room in the neighbourhood where I could store some of my collection. I simply had to clear books out. I tried donating books to select university libraries, but sadly, they weren't interested. Attempts to sell stuff weren't very successful either, so I ended up giving most of the books away. It's been awful. I don't want to give up on writing history altogether, and you never know what you might *need* in the way of references and sources.

There are parallels between clearing out libraries and bookshelves and clearing out wardrobes: maybe both are difficult for historians, who tend to value relics of the past and to assemble and to accumulate in order to understand. One salvages and needs records, texts and artefacts. Learning my craft in a pre-digital age, I acquired roomfuls of paperwork, old magazines, card-index systems, box files and books. I've been involved in a fair amount of conservation work over the years and have gone through countless battles to try to save and protect historic buildings. Those more dismissive of heritage often accuse conservationists of stuffiness, of an inability to let go of the past. Maybe there is something of an obsessiveness, a fear of loss in all this, as well as a genuine respect for the beauty of many older buildings and artefacts, and an appreciation of what we can learn from them.

Like getting rid of books, clearing out wardrobes can be a highly emotional experience. Those who have experienced sorting through the possessions of deceased relatives know this; clothes and shoes worn by someone loved or known well but no longer living can carry an unbearably poignant charge. Angela Carter's literary treatment of this theme was referred to in the previous chapter. One's own clothes, too, carry powerful associations. Again, Carter describes this well. In *Wise Children*, Dora Chance recalls her grandmother's disapproval of an early admirer of hers, who had tried to seduce her with a squirrel-skin fur coat. 'I've got it still,' Dora mused, 'it's in the big wardrobe in Grandma's room that we don't use any more, wrapped up in a white sheet, there's a ghost of antique Mitsouko clinging to the hairs, mothballs in one pocket, in the other the dehydrated skeleton of a gardenia left where I stuffed it, after a Certain Distinguished Person took it out of his buttonhole and slipped it down my cleavage.' Here there's nostalgia, a memory of lost youth, a rueful memory of her grandmother's principled disapproval of fur, a reminder of her love and protectiveness towards her granddaughters. The contents of a wardrobe can be charged with so many meanings and memories. They can also be disturbing, suggestive of a ghostly presence, not always benign. One recalls Daphne du Maurier's account of Mrs Danvers in *Rebecca*, in the sinister scene where the housekeeper pushes the hapless new Mrs de Winter into touching and feeling her dead predecessor's furs, velvets and lingerie. Rebecca's clothes carry a whiff of her scent, of white azalea flowers. Wine-coloured velvet, an ostrich feather fan wrapped in tissue paper, and 'a train of white satin, dripping on the floor of the wardrobe' suggest something visceral, as well as sensuous. 'I feel her everywhere,' intones the reptilian Mrs Danvers. 'Do you think the dead come back and watch the living?' The new Mrs de Winter shudders, can't swallow, and flees the room.

Wardrobes can be full of ghosts, as well as of poignant memories. Exploring the popular appeal of vintage clothes and artefacts in contemporary society, researcher Samantha Holland writes of *haunting*, the bodily traces and spectral remains found in old clothes. Some people react with revulsion at the idea of wearing cast-offs, or the clothing of the deceased. Others, less squeamish, may be motivated by ecological and social concerns; despair at the ubiquity of cheap, mass-produced clothing, sometimes manufactured in exploitative conditions, piling up waste on the planet. Then there are those who appreciate the beauty of, and exquisite craftsmanship which can be evident in, older clothing. The sense of garments as 'pre-loved' can give comfort, a sense of continuity through time. Lovers of vintage speak of 'authenticity', of respect for heritage, a love of the past. Some even feel that old clothes and intimate possessions are imbued with some kind of soul or spirit of their own.

I have felt all these things, and have experienced many contradictory emotions about old clothes. Writing about the history of glamour some years ago, I spent a good deal of time rooting around car boot sales and vintage fairs. There can be the sense of a treasure hunt, accompanied by the heady pleasures of serendipity; the possibility of discovering something wonderful. Even so, the musty smell and slightly tacky feel of old garments can stale enthusiasm. I explored collections of clothes in museums, where valuable items are often reverently wrapped in tissue paper and stored in acid-free cardboard boxes. On one occasion I asked to see a fur coat from the 1930s. The young assistant had to peel the tissue paper off, stained yellow through soaking up the lanoline in the animal skin: she was wearing gloves, but visibly shaken and revolted by what must have felt like unwrapping something corpse-like, like an Egyptian mummy.

CHAPTER EIGHTEEN

A trunk in the attic can be a boon for those not wanting to face a clear-out. But clothes stored this way, or pushed to the back of the wardrobe, can smell musty and remind one of the ravages of age. Now that I've made a start on clearing out my books, I know that I need to take on my wardrobe. Psychologically, I'm hugely resistant. Not only do I anticipate being unable to make decisions, but I am altogether uneasy about discovering what lurks at the back of the cupboards. I know that finding out will stir up memories and voices which are at present silted up, quiescent. Oh I can imagine! The tangles of silk and perished elastic of underwear that will bring to mind long-past love affairs. Those Tibetan boots garnished with gold braid and bright-coloured felt appliqué. I wore those, with tight black jeans and a loose black tunic, to parties in the late 1970s. There's a dress from the 1970s, too. Black jersey sprinkled with tiny brown leaves, cleverly cut and styled by 'Gill' for a label called Reflections, the lettering on the label curly and blobby and entirely reminiscent of that decade. That dress has a chequered history. It was consigned to my daughters' dressing-up box in the 1980s, and later claimed as vintage. After the girls left home, I reclaimed it. I tried it on again, not so long ago and it still fits. I'm not sure I'll ever wear it again now, but neither do I want to throw it out. Why? Probably because it documents who I was and what I felt good in some fifty years ago.

Then there's the red-and-black 1940s-shape sweater with the V-neck and slightly puffed sleeves that I have mentioned before. The wool under the arms is slightly matted now. Its label reminds me it was by Lee Bender for Bus Stop. I adored it. I felt so much myself, wearing it. And it reminds me that in the early 1970s I had a number of Lee Bender design sweaters of a similar shape, one or two of them wool, patterned in Fair Isle bands, another two with dramatic silver chevrons: one where the silver stripes alternated with black, the other, with scarlet. There's an example of one of the Fair Isle knitted sweaters in the V&A.

I remember that I wore mine to bits. The red-and-black Lee Bender sweater came from a boutique in Duke's Lane, Brighton. When I moved to Brighton in the 1970s, I was entranced by the number of boutiques: there had even, for a short while, been a branch of Biba.

I can't bring myself to throw out my Lee Bender sweater. So much else has gone. Recalling those Brighton boutiques in the 1970s starts me reminiscing all over again. There was a shop that sold long skirts and tunic tops crafted out of patchwork, using exquisite old fabrics, in gorgeous colours. Mine was in pale heliotrope georgette crêpe with bands of faded, floral-patterned silks. And I had a long skirt and matching top in dark, rose-patterned brocade which I remember wearing with raspberry-pink suede boots. I always liked toning and matching colours, until my daughters complained that I was 'too matchy-matchy', and in danger of looking like an air hostess.

What about the bits of old fur? Attitudes hardened towards the wearing of fur in the 1980s and 1990s, although there's no saving the animals who died a long time ago. I used to wear old fox furs from junk shops in my student days, they had heads on them with clasps to fasten round the neck, to join to tails. One fur scarf was a lovely golden brown, probably mink or marten. It didn't have a head, but the ends were finished in little tails. It was lined in a blonde tobacco-coloured silk, with exquisite stitching, ruched and scalloped at the edges. The silken cords for fastening it were finished with little brown silk acorns. Alas, it started to go a bit manky some years back, and it looked like bits were disintegrating, even turning into dust. So with some reluctance I consigned it to the rubbish bin. I still have a fur coat. I think it was originally described as 'coney', which I suppose is rabbit. My late husband bought it for me soon after we met. Maybe he thought that's what men should do, buy fur coats for their beloved. It would feel terribly disloyal to throw it out, though I don't wear it.

CHAPTER EIGHTEEN

So what *will* I throw out? The old silk underwear, definitely. Old, pale silk blouses, however exquisite the lace trim or embroidery. Silk and satin, even if they start off pearly as moonshine, tend to yellow with age, like old ivory, ancient molars or elephant tusks. Ugh: these can go. And surely I can get rid of some of the many, many black dresses that are shoehorned into the packed wardrobes? Some of them have worn bits and stains under the armpits, although they tend to be the ones I have enjoyed wearing the most. Jackets with eighties shoulder pads can go; I don't feel any affection for them at all. Shrivelled and perished swimsuits and bikinis: I hardly ever wear these and could do with updating them, if the need arises. All those coloured stockings and tights? Hmmm… another area where I might procrastinate, I fear, before piling stuff into the bin.

Shoes are one of the worst things. Age has brought me a bunion. It's no good, many of the shoes, however elegant or practical (I gave up on high heels decades ago), have to go.

Writing this has been a form of training, or preparation. I hope it won't have been a substitute for clearing out, a form of displacement therapy. I often think of a book that I read several decades ago by an American anthropological researcher, Marjorie Shostak, who spent time working with the !Kung people in the Kalahari Desert. She formed a particular bond with one older woman of the tribe, whom she called Nisa, and with whom she shared memories of many aspects of intimacy and life experiences. At some point in their relationship, Nisa told Marjorie that she would share the story of her life, then, 'like the others that have fallen out onto the sand' she would have done with it, would let it go. The wind would take it away. This seems to me very profound. I have shared something of my story through clothes. And now, many of the clothes still stuffed into corners of my wardrobes can be bundled into binbags and taken away.

References

CHAPTER ONE

Miller, J., *Crazy Age, Thoughts on Being Old* (London: Virago), 2010.

Athill, D., *Stet: A Memoir* (London: Granta), 2000; *Life Class: The Selected Memoirs of Diana Athill* (London: Granta), 2009; *Alive Alive Oh! And Other Things that Matter* (London: Granta), 2015.

Wilcox, C., *Patch Work: A Life Amongst Clothes* (London: Bloomsbury), 2020.

My love of clothes… I must discover: Bell, A.O., (ed.), *The Diary of Virginia Woolf*, vol. 3, 1925–30 (Harmondsworth: Penguin), 1987, entry for 14 May 1925, p. 21.

Goudge, E., *The Little White Horse* (London, University of London Press Ltd.), 1946.

Seton, A., *Dragonwyck* (London: Hodder and Stoughton), 1945.

Kennedy, M., *The Constant Nymph* (London: Heinemann), 1924.

Girls' Public Day School Trust… had refused: Dyhouse, C., *Girls Growing Up in Late Victorian and Edwardian England* (London: Routledge and Kegan Paul), 1981, p. 164.

In her absurd… punching bag of civilisation: Greer, G., *The Female Eunuch* (London: Paladin), 1971, p. 80.

struggle along dismal pavements… to sustain them: Tennant, E., *Girlitude: A Memoir of the 50s and 60s* (London: Jonathan Cape), 1999, p. 139.

covered in tiny thick starched lace frills… Victorian photograph quality: Drabble, M., *The Garrick Year* (Harmondsworth: Penguin), 1964, p. 44.

Balsdon, D., *Oxford Life* (London: Eyre and Spottiswoode) 1962, pp. 188–94. See also the same author's *The Day They Burned Miss Termag* (London: Eyre and Spottiswoode), 1961.

Alice Gardner… hat full of small change: Dyhouse, C., *Girl Trouble: Panic and Progress in the History of Young Women* (London: Zed Books), p. 52.

Enid Starkie **'in all the colours of the Rimbaud'**: Mitchell, L., *Maurice Bowra: A Life* (Oxford: Oxford University Press), 2010, p. 116.

REFERENCES

Dorothy Sayers… parrots in tiny gilt cages: Brittain, V., *The Women at Oxford: A Fragment of History* (London: Harrap and Co.), 1960, p.123.

Simmonds, P., *Mrs Weber's Diary* (London: Jonathan Cape), 1979.

clothing for women… climb up the professional ladder: Shulman, A., *Clothes… and Other Things that Matter* (London: Cassell), 2020, p. 55.

Grant, L., *The Thoughtful Dresser* (London: Virago), 2009.

Glendinning, V., *Rebecca West, A Life* (London: Weidenfeld and Nicolson), 1987, p. 62.

'the desperation of being sexy': Specter, M., in the New Yorker, 7 March 2004.

West, R., with an afterword by Glendinning, V., *Sunflower* (London: Virago), 1990, pp. 268–76.

John, A., *Elizabeth Robins; Staging a Life, 1862–1952* (London and New York: Routledge), 1995, p. 237.

For **Emily Tinne** see Rushton, P., *Mrs Tinne's Wardrobe: A Liverpool Lady's Clothes 1900–1940* (Liverpool: Bluecoat Press in Association with National Museums Liverpool), 2006. Linda Grant on Emily Tinne, *The Thoughtful Dresser*, pp. 66–67.

CHAPTER TWO

marvels of fashion pornography: Showalter, E., 'Emeralds on the Home Front', the *Guardian*, 10 August 2002.

For Stafford Cripps opposition to New Look, see Higgins, C., 'V&A takes fresh look at New Look that swept away the postwar blues', the *Guardian*, 16 March 2007; Alison Settle, *Notes on Fashion in the War Years*, 1939–1946, unpublished typescript (reference B 405.5) in Alison Settle Collection, Design Archive, University of Brighton.

No Store Buyer… decorated with pearls: Settle, A., 'Coronation Lead to Couture', the *Observer*, 3 August 1952.

Steedman, C., *Landscape for a Good Woman: A Story of Two Lives* (London: Virago), 1986, p. 24.

a froth of cream, delicate pink and white chiffon: Gallico, P., *Flowers for Mrs Harris* (London: Michael Joseph), 1958, pp. 85–86.

American women making on average about twelve dresses per year in Settle, A., the *Observer*, 3 August 1952.

For **Horrockses Fashions** see Boydell, C., *Horrockses Fashions: Off-the-Peg style in the '40s and '50s*, also Settle, A., 'A Woman's Viewpoint', the *Observer*, 22 November 1953.

in a white room, trellised with velvety red roses: Settle, A., 'A Woman's Viewpoint', the *Observer*, 1 June 1952.

the poured in look: Settle, A., in the *Observer*, 3 August 1952.

fashion show in Hampstead: Settle, A., 'A Woman's Viewpoint', the *Observer*, 22 November 1953.

CHAPTER THREE

unsuitable ornamentation: Ridley, A.E., *Frances Mary Buss and Her Work for Education* (London: Longmans, Green & Co.), 1896

The gymslip… 1920s: Mary Tait, a pupil of Swedish gymnastic pioneer Madame Bergman-Österberg, is generally credited with the invention of the gymslip.

The GFS… the 1930s: Dyhouse, C., *Girl Trouble*, p. 34.

The story goes… along with the boys: Dyhouse, C., *Girl Trouble*, pp. 72–73.

Guides' uniform details from Kerr, R., *The Story of the Girl Guides* (London: Girl Guides Association with Stanhope Press), 1932.

Contemporary accounts show… better days: Kerr, R., *Story of the Girl Guides*, p. 64.

Princesses Elizabeth and Margaret as Guides: British Pathé film, https://www.britishpathe.com/asset/82566/

Marshall, A., *Girls Will be Girls* (London: Hamish Hamilton), 1974; *Giggling in the Shrubbery* (London: HarperCollins), 1985.

For **St Trinian's cartoon schoolgirls** see *Ronald Searle: Graphic Master* (London: Cartoon Museum), 2010. Posy Simmonds' comments, p. 155.

For **Judith Okely schooling** see her essay 'Privileged, Schooled and Finished: Boarding Education for Girls', in Ardener, S., *Defining Females: The Nature of Women in Society* (London: Routledge), 1993.

Mary Evans schooling: Evans, M., *A Good School: Life at a Girls' Grammar School in the 1950s* (London: The Women's Press), 1991.

In the memoir… cost of the uniform: Wilmott, P., *A Green Girl* (London: Peter Owen), 1983.

'lisle stockings were for ladies': Gamble, R., *Chelsea Child* (London: BBC/Ariel Books), 1979, p. 165.

Government Guidance on School Uniform: Department of Education, 19 November 2021.

CHAPTER FOUR

Reveille: Life-size cut-out photo of Brigitte Bardot featured in issue for 31 October 1957.

Alan Dent… 'fondlesome kittens': in *The Illustrated London News*, 23 March 1957, p. 33.

curvy little craft with crafty little curves: Donald Zec in the *Daily Mirror*, 13 July 1957, p. 7.

For **first liberated woman of postwar France** see Poirier, A., 'Happy Birthday, Brigitte Bardot' in the *Guardian,* 22 September 2009. https://www.theguardian.com/film/2009/sep/22/brigitte-bardot-french-cinema (accessed 23 January 2024).

REFERENCES

hunter as much as prey: de Beauvoir, S., *Brigitte Bardot and the Lolita Syndrome*, originally *Esquire*, 1 August 1959, republished by Four Square Books, New English Library, 1960.

In the Latin countries… mutual desire and pleasure: *Brigitte Bardot and the Lolita Syndrome*.

French journalist… undermining the bourgeoisie: Poirier, 'Happy Birthday Brigitte Bardot'.

According to the *Daily Mail*… in Nice and following comments on Gillian Hills: from Mulchrone, V., 'That Bardot Look' in the *Daily Mail*, 11 December 1958; Tanfield, P., 'Is Doing a Bardot Fair to a 14-Year-Old Schoolgirl?', the *Daily Mail*, 28 January 1959.

CHAPTER FIVE

Greene and Gordon comments on *Lolita*; Connolly, Julian W., 'The Creation of Lolita', *A Reader's Guide to Nabokov's "Lolita"*, Academic Studies Press, 2009, pp. 3–8. *JSTOR*, https://www.jstor.org/stable/j.ctt1zxsk0k (accessed 23 January 2024).

Paul Tanfield in the *Daily Mail*, 'Is Doing a Bardot Fair to a 14-Year-Old Schoolgirl?', the *Daily Mail*, 28 January 1959.

As early as 1956… duffel coat and jeans: Settle, A., 'Viewpoint', the *Observer*, 12 February 1956.

Fashion journalist Phyllis Heathcote… saying so: the *Guardian*, 28 February 1958.

In her 1959 essay… '*femme fatale*': de Beauvoir, S., *Brigitte Bardot and the Lolita Syndrome*, originally *Esquire*, 1 August 1959, republished by Four Square Books, New English Library, 1960.

Mark Abrams on teenage spending: *The Teenage Consumer*, London Press Exchange, Report no. 5, July 1959.

Barbara Hulanicki… judgement: Hulanicki, B., *From A to Biba* (London: V&A Publishing), 2007, p. 100.

Riviere, J., 'Womanliness as Masquerade,' *International Journal of Psychoanalysis*, 10, pp. 303–13.

A fashion feature… to contemporary attitudes: 'The Brain Bunnies', *Honey* Magazine, no. 79, October 1966.

The mind-body problem… rigorous conflict: Byatt, A., 'Soul Searching', the *Guardian*, 14 February 2004.

CHAPTER SIX

Be deeply thankful… fussy, ugly, overdone: Settle, A., *Clothes Line* (London: Methuen), 1937, p. 137.

Approaching sixty… reasonableness: Horwell, V., Obituary of Margot Smyly, the *Guardian*, 11 June 2005.

For many girls… oozed class: on this theme see Moseley, R., *Growing Up with Audrey Hepburn* (Manchester: Manchester University Press), 2002.

For **Holly Golightly as an 'American geisha'** see Halford, M., 'Was Holly Golightly Really a Prostitute?' in *The New Yorker*, 7 September 2009.

We had to put a stop to it…. Every tart in London was getting in: quoted by MacCarthy, F., *Last Curtsey; The End of the Debutantes* (London: Faber and Faber), 2006, p. 14.

The sixties began… about to boil: Carter, E., *With Tongue in Chic* (London: Michael Joseph), 1974, p. 140.

Vogue* replaced Mrs Exeter… Not *Vogue: Muir, R., 'Behind the Legend of Mrs Exeter, Vogue's First Grey Haired Star', *Vogue*, 13 September 2020.

After the First World War… from what women wore: Priestley, J.B., *English Journey* (London: Heinemann), 1934, p. 401; Orwell, G., *The Road to Wigan Pier* (Harmondsworth: Penguin), 1972 (1937), p. 79. Burke, T., *London in My Time* (London: Rich and Cowan), 1934, pp. 65–66. See also Dyhouse, C., *Glamour: Women, History, Feminism* (London: Zed Books), 2010, p. 72, for general discussion of this.

CHAPTER SEVEN

'America's best known clothing consultant': Molloy, J.T., *The Woman's Dress for Success Book* (Chicago: Follett Publishing Company) 1977. The quotations that follow are from this source.

For **Miss Lorimer 'put on her hat' to confront the young men** see Frisella, E., 'Go Home and Sit Still: World War I and Women's Colleges at Oxford' in *Isis*, 2 March 2015.

For **Mrs Thatcher's wedding outfit** see Conway, D., 'Margaret Thatcher, Dress and the Politics of Fashion' in Behnke, A., *The International Politics of Fashion: Being Fab in a Dangerous World* (London: Routledge), 2016.

'a pale grey Cerruti number with a fine pale blue stripe': this and following quotations from Shulman, A., *Clothes… and other things that matter* (London: Cassell), 2021, pp. 51–57.

leather trousers: Ferrier, M., 'Theresa May's Leather Trousers: You need a tough hide to wear them': in the *Guardian*, 7 December 2016.

For **Part of her success… focus on dress and appearance** see Morrissey, H., *Style and Substance: A Guide for Women who Want to Win at Work* (London: Piatkus), 2021, especially chapters 1 and 3.

CHAPTER EIGHT

Mass Observation Report on the New Look, March 1949, 3095, Mass Observation (MO) Archive, The Keep, Brighton.

the bottom of the ladder... who don't own a diamond: Harrisson, T., typescript, 'Mass Observation and the Masses' Hats', MO Topic 18 Box 5, MO Archive, The Keep, Brighton.

Mass Observers asked people... 'didn't know or care': MO Topic 18 5/B.

They sometimes got riled by MO questioning: MO Topic 18 Box 2: a twenty-seven-year-old woman in Burdett Road.

Mass Observation Spring Directive on Clothes, 1988: The Keep, Brighton. Material on following pages from this source.

Viv herself was aware... 'messes with their heads. Good': quotations from Albertine, V., *Clothes, Music, Boys: A Memoir* (London: Faber & Faber), 2015, pp. 111–12.

Buckley, C., and Fawcett, H., *Fashioning the Feminine: Representation and Women's Fashion from the Fin de Siècle to the Present* (London: I.B. Tauris), 2001.

CHAPTER NINE

During the coronavirus pandemic... reported shopping more online: UK: change in online shopping since COVID-19 2020–2021, Statista

On **Pryce Jones** see Whaley, S., 'The Pryce was Right' in *Best of British* Magazine, December 2021; Coopey, R., O'Connell, S., and Porter, D., *Mail Order Retailing in Britain: A Business and Social History* (Oxford: Oxford University Press), 2005.

For **One recent history... posh department store** see Mann, J., 'The Pattern of Mail Order', in *European Journal of Marketing,* January 1967, pp. 42–53.

For store catalogues from 1950s see https://www.vintagecatalogues.com.

Baroness Morrissey on Instagram Helena Morrissey (@helenamorrissey) Instagram photos and videos (accessed 26 March 2024).

For **Helena Morrissey... Covid pandemic** see Morrissey, H., *Style and Substance*, pp. 211–12.

CHAPTER TEN

Glamour is a slithery concept... through time: Dyhouse, C., *Glamour: Women, History, Feminism*, esp. p. 162 ff.

When Mass Observers... 'flash' dressing: MO Spring Directive on Clothes, 1988, The Keep.

In Britain, the radical politician Claudia Jones... women in London: Dyhouse, C., *Glamour,* pp. 129–31.

For **In 1908, literary scholar Edith Morley...not treated her kindly** see Dyhouse, C., *No Distinction of Sex? Women in British Universities 1870–1945* (London: UCL Press), 1995, pp. 156–61.

One year I discovered... the Women's Co-Operative Guild in 1915: Women's Co-Operative Guild, *Letters from Working Women* (London: G. Bell), 1915.

American feminist Susan Faludi... backlash against the feminism of the 1970s: Faludi, S., *Backlash: The Undeclared War against Women* (London: Chatto and Windus), 1991.

But an uncompromising attack... never going to have widespread appeal: Bartky, S., *Femininity and Domination: Studies in the Phenomenology of Oppression* (New York and London: Routledge), 1990, pp. 36–42; Dyhouse, C., *Glamour*, pp. 59–60.

Jane Walsh... swagger a little, wearing it: Walsh, J., *Not Like This* (London: Lawrence and Wishart), 1953, p. 31.

Joan Wyndham... found in Woolworths: Wyndham, J., *Love Lessons* (London: Virago), 2001, p. 30.

Nerina Shute... more natural look: Shute, N., *We Mixed Our Drinks* (London: Jarrolds), 1945, p. 87.

CHAPTER ELEVEN

Luca Turin on Je Reviens: 'Accords and Discords: Perfume Reviews' in Drobnick, J.(ed.), *The Smell Culture Reader* (Oxford: Berg), 2006, p. 221.

Susan Irvine... 'new leather handbag': Irvine, S., *The Perfume Guide* (London: Haldane Mason), 2000, p. 115.

Psychologist and perfume specialist Joachim Mensing... power in sexual politics: quoted by Rankin, Diana, in 'Perfume Names through the Ages', posted 21 August 2020, https://perfumepower.co.za (accessed 8 March 2023).

common, real Woolworths, even for us: Hoggart, R., *Everyday Language and Everyday Life* (London: Transaction Publishers), 2003, p. 80.

perfume is a language close to the unconscious: reference to Giacobetti in Herman, B., *Scent and Subversion; Decoding a Century of Provocative Perfume* (Guilford, Connecticut: Lyons Press), 2013, p. 13.

CHAPTER TWELVE

One of my earliest... button tin: for an extended exploration of similar experience see Knight, L., *The Button Box* (London: Vintage), 2016.

For **Snowdrop Bands** see Dyhouse, C., *Girls Growing Up*, pp. 109–10.

Art Historian Marcia Pointon... working in hair: Pointon, M., *Wearing Memory: Mourning, Jewellery and the Body*, in Ecker, Gisela, *Trauer tragen – Trauer zeigen; Inszenierungen der Geschlechter* (Wilhelm Fink Verlag: 1999).

Clip-on spectacle adornments: advertised in *Costume Jewellery & Fashion Accessories* (Trade Magazine), no. 3, 1955.

REFERENCES

CHAPTER THIRTEEN

Sharp-eyed Mass Observers… thirteen years of age: MO Topic 18, Box 2, File I/F, The Keep, Brighton. See especially section on 'The contents of a girl's handbag'.

Friday Night is Amami Night: Amami shampoo was popular between the wars and heavily advertised, the adverts suggesting that women bonded over hairwashing and beauty routines on a Friday night before going out over the weekend.

Helena Rubinstein… beauty mask… slices of raw beef: Dyhouse, C., *Glamour*, p.19.

Political and Economic Planning (PEP), Vol. XXIV, no. 425, *Modern Cosmetics and Perfumery*, 25 August 1958.

For **Woolworths' new 'Baby Doll' range** see 'Brand Profile: Baby Doll Cosmetics', 30 August 2021, https://www.makeupmuseum.org/home/2021/08/baby-doll-cosmetics.html (accessed 8 March 2023)

Angela Carter's descriptions of Fevvers: Carter, A., *Nights at the Circus* (London: Chatto and Windus), 1984.

Merriam, E., *Figleaf: The Business of Being in Fashion* (Philadelphia and New York: Lippincott), 1960.

Peiss, K., *Hope in a Jar: The Making of America's Beauty Culture* (New York: Henry Holt), 1998.

CHAPTER FOURTEEN

Horrockses-style sundresses: for further reading see Boydell, C., *Horrockses Fashions: Off-the-Peg Style in the '40s and '50s* (London: V&A Publishing), 2010.

Steedman, Carolyn, *Landscape for a Good Woman: A Story of Two Lives* (London: Virago) 1986, pp. 37, 38.

CHAPTER FIFTEEN

This chapter is based on the answers to an open-ended questionnaire completed for me by my daughters, Alex and Eugénie von Tunzelmann. I am extremely grateful for their help in this.

CHAPTER SIXTEEN

Rebecca West… luxuries from expensive shops: Glendinning, V., *Rebecca West: A Life* (London: Weidenfeld and Nicolson), 1987, p. 62.

the constant interplay between love and the desire for clothes: Ernaux, A., *Getting Lost* (London: Fitzcarraldo Editions), 2022, p. 25.

when I continually bought skirts… spending as if there were no tomorrow: Ernaux A., *Getting Lost*, p. 25.

clothes would be glimpsed only briefly… heap on the floor: Ernaux, A., *Simple Passion* (London: Fitzcarraldo Editions), 2021, p.17.

a brilliantly detailed account… for so little reward: Albertine, V., *To Throw Away Unopened* (London: Faber & Faber), 2019, pp. 245–50.

like two milky jellyfish trawled up from Dungeness beach: *Ibid.,* p. 247.

In a 2022 case in Kerala, for instance… 'provocatively': https://thewire.in/law/womans-provocative-dress-cannot-give-licence-to-a-man-to-outrage-her-modesty-kerala-hc (accessed 9 March 2023).

Charlie Porter unpicks: Porter, C., *Bring No Clothes: Bloomsbury and the Philosophy of Fashion* (London: Particular Books, Penguin Random House), 2023, p. 149 ff.

For **the Victorian obsession with corsets and tight lacing** see Steele, V., *The Corset: A Cultural History* (New Haven and London: Yale University Press) 2001.

Miuccia Prada… fashion intellectual: 'Miuccia Prada: An Intellectual with Dress Sense', the *Guardian,* 1 November 2012.

https://www.theguardian.com/fashion/2020/oct/30/miuccia-prada-fashion-politics-architecture (accessed 9 March 2023).

Too rich a dress may sometimes check desire: Ovid, *Ars Amatoria*, Book 3.

true eroticism is transgressive: Rodgers, D., 'Five Times Prada Made Ugly Sexy' *Dazed*, 25 February 2021.

https://www.dazeddigital.com/fashion/article/52026/1/miuccia-prada-ugly-sexy-fashion-big-pants-socks-sandals-aw21-show-raf-simons (accessed 9 March 2023).

In 1917, a young Rebecca West wrote… to sensuous delights: from *Selected Letters of Rebecca West*, edited by Bonnie Kime Scott (New Haven: Yale University Press), 2001.

CHAPTER SEVENTEEN

silk, satin, lace… uplift bras: Carter, A., *Wise Children* (London: Vintage) 2006, p. 187.

A history of the world in party frocks: Carter, A., *Wise Children*, p. 187.

Clothes are a lifelong journey into acquiring an identity: Grant, L., *The Thoughtful Dresser* (London: Virago), 2009, p. 162.

Beckerman, I., *Love, Loss and What I Wore* (Chapel Hill, North Carolina: Algonquin Books), 1995.

The cool fur brush… satin and fur and skin: Wilcox, C., *Patch Work,* p.138, **marvellous tonic to the senses**: *ibid.*, p. 129.

Dress has never been at all… attaches to it: Bowen, E., review of Willett Cunningham, C., *English Women's Clothing in the Nineteenth Century*, in *Collected Impressions* (London: Longmans Green and Co), 1950, pp. 111–15.

It's impossible to imagine the women's movement dressed in the New Look: Grant, L., *Thoughtful Dresser*, p. 157.

On the 1950s and its contradictions for women's history see Tinkler, P., Spencer, S., and Langhamer, C. (eds) *Women in Fifties Britain: A New Look* (London: Routledge), 2019.

Thrown back among… fantasies: Bowen, E., review of Willett Cunningham, C., p. 112.

Horwood, C., *Keeping Up Appearances: Fashion and Class Between the Wars* (Stroud: Sutton Publishing), 2005.

Writers J.B. Priestley and Thomas Burke: Priestley, J. B., *English Journey* (London: Heinemann) 1934, p. 401; Burke, T., *London in My Time* (London: Rich and Cowan), 1934, pp. 65–66; **daydreams of themselves as Greta Garbo**: Orwell, G., *The Road to Wigan Pier* (Harmondsworth: Penguin), 1972 (1937), p. 79.

when we dress… personal psychology and the social order: Wilson, E., *Adorned in Dreams: Fashion and Modernity* (London: Virago), 1985, p. 247.

CHAPTER EIGHTEEN

she would not lose one memory… dated and complete: Strachey, L., *Life of Queen Victoria* (New York: Harcourt, Brace and Co), 1921, p. 399.

I Murdered my Library: Grant, L., the *Guardian*, 17 May 2014.

It's in the big wardrobe… slipped it down my cleavage: Carter, A., *Wise Children,* p. 92.

Daphne du Maurier's account of Mrs Danvers: *Rebecca* (London: Virago), 2003, pp. 190–94.

Samantha Holland writes of *haunting*: Holland, S., *Modern Vintage Homes & Leisure Lives: Ghosts and Glamour* (London: Palgrave Macmillan), 2018.

like the others that have fallen out onto the sand: Shostak, M., *Nisa: The Life and Words of a !Kung Woman* (London: Earthscan Publications), 1990, epigraph.

Acknowledgements

I owe thanks to all those writers and scholars whose work is mentioned in these pages. And to the many people who have helped me, sometimes inadvertently, to complete this book. I can't name them all. But I'm grateful for encouragement, and for conversations about writing and publishing, to Maggie Hanbury, Helen Taylor, Jeanne Openshaw, Jim Burge, Mick Hamer and Stephanie Pain. Warm thanks, too, for long-term inspiration and support from Hester Barron, Claire Langhamer and Marcia Pointon. Vincent Quinn is someone whose understanding, kindness and sagacity I have come to rely on a great deal in recent times. Jenny Shaw and I have shared countless conversations about clothes in the past and my thanks to her for her insights and for her friendship. My friendships with Helen Taylor, Madge Dresser and Ulrike Hanna Meinhof go back decades, and have always been an important source of strength. More recently, it has been a great pleasure to work with the team at Unicorn Publishing, and I am grateful, particularly, to Lucy Duckworth, Imogen Palmer, Ramona Lamport and Felicity Price-Smith for their friendly and cooperative – as well as highly skilled and creative work. Stephen Buckley, discerning and generous, has been brilliant in so many ways. And particular thanks, of course, to Alex and Eugénie von Tunzelmann, for freely sharing ideas, and for always having been a source of joy and inspiration.

Picture Credits

Many thanks to the following institutions for images:
p. 43 courtesy of The Land of Lost Content Collection/Mary Evans Picture Library
p. 44 Chronicle/Alamy Stock Photo
p. 57 Advertising Archives
pp. 60-1 © British Library Board, [LOU.LON 88]
p. 69 Reg Speller / Stringer
p. 74 Retro AdArchives/Alamy Stock Photo
p. 81 Advertisement for EMBA mink from J.G. Links, *The Book of Fur,* James Barrie 1956
p. 89 Mary Evans/APL
p. 99 Ken Russell/TopFoto
p.101 © Estate of Shirley Baker/Mary Evans Picture Library
p. 119 Advertising Archives
p. 144 Retro AdArchives/Alamy Stock Photo
All other images are courtesy of the author.

Every effort has been made to trace and contact all copyright holders; if notified, the publisher will rectify any errors or omissions at the earliest possibility.

Index

A

Abrams, Mark, 71
Addams, Wednesday, 28
Albertine, Viv, 101–2, 176–7
Alexandra, Queen, 136
Amies, Hardy, 44
Amini, Mahsa, 179
And God Created Woman (film, 1956), 60, 63
anti-fashion, 98
Archer, Margaret Scotford, 112
Arden, Elizabeth, 143
Athill, Diana, 7

B

Baby Doll (film, 1956), 67, 70
'baby-doll look', 68–9
Baden-Powell, Agnes, 51
Baden-Powell, Robert, 51
Balcon, Michael, 39
Balsdon, Dacre, 25
Bardot, Brigitte, 59–65, 70
Bartky, Sandra Lee, 115
Beat Girl (film, 1960), 63–4
Beatnik Beauty (film, 1963), 64–5
beatnik style, 64
Beauvoir, Simone de, 'Brigitte Bardot and the Lolita Syndrome' (1959), 61–3, 69–70
Beaux, Ernest (parfumier), 118
Beckerman, Ilene, *Love, Loss and What I Wore* (2005), 183–4
Biba, 22, 65, 71, 100, 146
Birtwell, Celia, 100
Bjelland, Kat, 100
Blake, Peter, 60
Bowen, Elizabeth, 185, 187–8
Bowra, Maurice, 26
Brazil, Angela, 50
Breakfast at Tiffany's (film, 1958), 78–9, 136
Brent-Dyer, Elinor, 50
British Social Attitudes Survey, 83
Brittain, Vera, 12
Brontë, Charlotte, *Jane Eyre*, 48
Brontë sisters, 48
Brooke, Simon, 124
Brooks, Louise, 136
Bruce, Dorita Fairlie, 50
Buckley, Cheryl, 102
Buer, Mabel, 112
Burke, Thomas, 188
Buss, Frances, 49
Byatt, Antonia, 75

C

Cameron, David, 92
Capote, Truman, 78–9
Carlyle, Rachel, 191
Carter, Angela:
    Nights at the Circus, 145
    Wise Children (1991), 182–3, 193
Carter, Ernestine, 82
Chanel:
    nail varnish, 146
    perfumes, 118
Chanel, Coco, 136
Charlot, Juli Lynne, 44
cinema, influence on fashion, 39–40
circle skirts, 44–5

Clark, Ossie, 22, 100
clothing rations, in the Second World War, 8
contraceptive pill, 72
cosmetics: marketing of, 142–5
  see also make-up
Coty (perfume house), 126–7
Covid-19 pandemic, 92, 103, 107, 123, 166
Crawford, Carole Joan, 112
Creed, Charles, 44
crinolines, 36–9
Cripps, Sir Stafford, 40
Cunningham, C. Willett, 185

D

Dahl, Sophie, 128
Davies, Emily, 86
Davis, Fred, *Fashion, Culture and Identity* (1992), 98
Deneuve, Catherine, 60
Dent, Alan, 60
Devil Wears Prada, The (film, 2006), 90
Dietrich, Marlene, 31, 61, 109
Dior (fashion house), 38, 40–4, 94
Disraeli, Benjamin, 132
Dors, Diana, 110
Drabble, Margaret, *The Garrick Year*, 18
Dresser, Madge, 23
Du Maurier, Daphne, *Rebecca*, 193–4

E

Education Act (1944), 82
Elizabeth, Queen (*later* Queen Mother), 38
Elizabeth II, Queen, 42, 52, 110
  wedding, 41
Empire Stores mail-order catalogue, 105
Ernaux, Annie, 175–6
'Essex Girl', 84
Evans, Mary, 55
Evans, Valerie, 68

F

Faludi, Susan, 114
Fanny by Gaslight (1944), 40
Fawcett, Hilary, 102
feminism, second-wave, 111, 113–15, 141
Ferrier, Morwenna, 92
Flechier, Edouard, 122
flowers, language of, 132
Fonda, Jane, 60
Forever Amber (film, 1947), 39
Forster, E.M., 178
Forster, Flora Macrae, 12–14

G

Gainsborough studios, 39–40
Gallico, Paul, *Flowers for Mrs Harris*, 41, 186
Gamble, Rose, 56
Garbo, Greta, 109
Gardner, Alice, 25–6
Garbo, Greta, 109
Gardner, Alice, 25–6
Gigi (film, 1958), 78
Girl Guides, 51–2
Girls' Friendly Society, 51
Girls Public Day School Company, 49
girls' school stories, 50–1, 54
Givenchy, Hubert de, 78
'Glamazons', 88, 91
glamour, 109–16
Glendinning, Victoria, *Rebecca West: A Life*, 31–4
Goebbels, Joseph, 47
Gone with the Wind (film, 1939), 39
Gordon, John, 67
Goudge, Elizabeth, *The Little White Horse*, 9
Grant, Linda:
  'I Murdered my Library,' 192
  The Thoughtful Dresser, 31, 35, 183, 186, 187
Greco, Juliette, 64
Green, Felicity, 65
Greene, Graham, 67

Greer, Germaine, *The Female Eunuch*, 14
Greville, Edmond T., 63
Griffe, Jacques, 66
Grossmith (perfume house), 123–4
grunge, 100–2
Guerlain perfumes, 122

H

Haffenden, Elizabeth, 40
Harlow, Jean, 109
Harrisson, Tom, 95
Hartnell, Norman, 38
Head, Edith, 78
Heathcote, Phyllis, 68
Hepburn, Audrey, 78–9, 136
Hills, Gillian, 63, 67
Hoggart, Richard, 124
Holland, Mary, 151
Holland, Samantha, 194
Hollywood, 109–10
Honey (magazine), 71, 73, 75, 145
Horrockses Fashions, 42, *43*, *44*
Horsburgh, Florence, 54
Horwood, Catherine, *Keeping Up Appearances* (2005), 188
Hosten, Jennifer, 111
Hulanicki, Barbara, 65, 70, 71, 100
Hurley, Elizabeth, 102

I

I Don't Know How She Does It (film, 2011), 90
internet: influence on fashion, 107–8
see also online shopping
social media
Irvine, Susan, 121

J

Jackie (magazine), 145
Janet Reger, 30
Jennings, Humphrey, 95
jewellery:
 1950s, 130–1
 jet, 133–4
 meaning of gemstones, 132–3
 pearls, 136–7
 social and cultural associations, 135–7
John, Angela, 34
Jones, Claudia, 112
Jourdan True Charm (perfume house), 127

K

Kardashian, Kim, 185
Keeler, Christine, 20
Kennedy, Margaret, 12
Klein, Viola, 112
Kondo, Marie, 190

L

Laroche, Guy, 66
Le Cain, Errol, 28
Leigh, Vivien, 39
Lévy, Raoul, 60
Littlewoods mail-order catalogue, 105
Lorimer, Hilda, 87
Love, Courtney, 100
Lucie Clayton schools, 110

M

Mad Men (TV series), 45
Mädchen in Uniform (film, 1931), 47–8
Madge, Charles, 95
Madonna (singer), 30, 100
Madonna of the Seven Moons (1945), 40
Magnusson, Margareta, 190
mail-order catalogues, 103–6
Mair, Carolyn, 191
make-up, 138–47
Malle, Louis, 63
Man in Grey, The (film, 1943), 40
Mansfield, Jayne, 110
Marcus, Laura, 116
Margaret, Princess, 40, 44, 52, 80
Marshall, Arthur, 54
Marshall Ward mail-order catalogue, 105

INDEX

Mass Observation (MO), 94–8, 111, 138
maternity clothes, 27
May, Theresa, 91–2
Mensing, Joachim, 122
Merriam, Eve, 147
Miller, Jane, 7
miniskirts, 100
Miss World competition (1970), 111–12
Mitchell, Juliet, 112
modesty, and women's clothing, 178–9
Molloy, John T., *The Woman's Dress for Success Book* (1977), 85–6, 87–8
Molyneux, Edward, 42
Molyneux, Kathleen, 42
Monroe, Marilyn, 154, 185
Morgan, Nicky, 92
Morley, Edith, 112
Morrissey, Helena (Baroness Morrissey), *Style and Substance* (2021), 92, 106–7
Morton, Alastair, 42
Morton, Digby, 44
Motion Picture Production (Hays) Code, 110
Muir, Robin, 82
My Fair Lady (film, 1964), 78

N

Nabokov, Vladimir, *Lolita*, 62, 66–7, 70
New Look, 38, 40–4, 94
North London Collegiate School, 49

O

Okely, Judith, 55
online shopping, 103, 106
Opium (perfume), 128
Orbach, Susie, *Fat is a Feminist Issue* (1979), 114
Orwell, George, 83, 188
Ovid (Latin poet), 180
Oxenham, Elsie, 50

P

Paolozzi, Eduardo, 42
pearl jewellery, 136–7
Pearson, Allison, 90
Peiss, Kathy, *Hope in a Jar* (1998), 147
perfume, 117–28
Philip, Prince (Duke of Edinburgh), 41
Phul–Nana (perfume), 123–4
Plunkett, Walter, 39
Pointon, Marcia, 133
Poirier, Agnès, 63
Pollock, Alice, 100
Porter, Charlie, 178
power dressing, 30, 87–93
Prada, Miuccia, 32, 175, 180–1
Priestley, J. B., 83, 188
Primrose League, The, 132
'Princess line', 42–4
Pryce Jones, 103–4
punk, influence on fashion, 100–2

Q

Quant, Mary, 70, 100, 145
Quorum, 100

R

restrictions, on women's clothing, 178–9
Reveille (newspaper), 60, 69
Rhodes, Zandra, 102
Rice-Davies, Mandy, 20
Riot Grrrls (band), 100
Rivière, Joan, 'Womanliness as Masquerade' (1928–29), 72
Robins, Elizabeth, 34
Rodgers, Daniel, 181
Roman Holiday (film, 1953), 78
Roudnitska, Edmond, 121
Rubinstein, Helena, 143
Russell, Ken, 98–9

S

'Sabrina' (Norma Ann Sykes), 110
Sabrina Fair (film, 1954), 78
Sagan, Leontine, 47
Sayers, Dorothy, 26
school uniforms:
    cost, 56–8
    fetishisation of, 55
    history of, 46–54
    requirements, 11–12
Scott, Sir Walter, 109
Searle, Ronald, 54–5
Seton, Anya, *Dragonwyck*, 11
Settle, Alison, 41–4, 66–8, 76–7
Seven Year Itch, The (film, 1955), 154
Sex Discrimination Act (1975), 22
Sex Kittens Go to College (film, 1960), 75
Shostak, Marjorie, 197
Showalter, Elaine, 39
Shrimpton, Jean, 82
Shulman, Alexandra, 30, 90
Shute, Nerina, 115–16
Simmonds, Posy, 28, 55
Slaughter, Audrey, 71
Slimane, Heidi, 102
Slits (band), 176
    Typical Girls, 101
Smyly, Margot, 77
'Snowdrop Bands', 132
social class, and dress, 76–84
social media, and selfies, 106–7
Soir de Paris (perfume), 118, 126
Solihull High School for Girls, 12
Spare Rib (magazine), 141
Spitting Image (TV series), 88
St Laurent, Yves, 66, 102, 121–2
Starkic, Enid, 26
Steedman, Carolyn, 41, 150–1
Stenton, Lady Doris, 21
Stiebel, Victor, 44
Strachey, Lytton, 190–1
Stroyberg, Annette, 59–60
Sutherland, Graham, 42
Swinging London, 82

T

Tanfield, Paul, 67
Taylor, Helen, 23
Teddy Girls, 98–9
Tennant, Emma, *Girlitude*, 17
Thatcher, Margaret, 87–8
Thorp, Nicola, 91
Tinne, Emily, 34–5
Travilla, William, 154
Tullis, John, 42
Tunzelmann, Alex von, 157–74
Tunzelmann, Eugénie von, 157–74
Tunzelmann, Nick von, 24, 159
Turin, Luca, 120–1

U

university education for women, 72–5, 86–7

V

V&A Museum, 184–5
Vadim, Roger, 59, 63
Versace, 102
Victoria, Queen, 190–1
vintage clothing, 194
Vogue (magazine), 77, 82, 88, 90, 165

W

Wakeley, Amanda, 92
Walsh, Jane, 115
West, Mae, 109
West, Rebecca, 31, 33, 175, 181
Westwood, Vivienne, 32, 100
Whitby, Yorkshire, jet industry, 133
Wicked Lady, The (1945), 40
Wilberforce, Octavia, 34
Wilcox, Claire, *Patch Work: A Life Amongst Clothes*, 8, 184–5
Williams, Tennessee, 67, 70
Willmott, Phyllis, *A Green Girl*, 56
Wilson, Elizabeth, *Adorned in Dreams* (1985), 188
Wolf, Naomi, *The Beauty Myth* (1990), 114

Women's Junior Air Corps (WJAC),
   52–4
women's liberation movement, 111
Woolf, Virginia, 7–8
Wyndham, Joan, 115

Y

Youthquake, 81–2, 100, 143

Z

Zec, Donald, 60

Published in 2025 by Unicorn
an imprint of Unicorn Publishing Group
Charleston Studio
Meadow Business Centre
Lewes BN8 5RW
www.unicornpublishing.org

Text © Carol Dyhouse
Images © see Picture Credits, p. 209

All rights reserved. No part of the contents of this book may be reproduced, stored in or introduced into a retrieval system, or transmitted, in any form or by any means (electronic, mechanical, photocopying, recording or otherwise), without the prior written permission of the copyright holder and the above publisher of this book.

Every effort has been made to trace copyright holders and to obtain their permission for the use of copyright material. The publisher apologises for any errors or omissions and would be grateful if notified of any corrections that should be incorporated in future reprints or editions of this book.

ISBN 978-1-916846-68-5
10 9 8 7 6 5 4 3 2 1

Design by Felicity Price-Smith
Printed in Malta by Gutenberg Press Ltd

Praise for Appearances

'Riveting – at once an innovative and intensely readable, personal memoir and a sharply-observed piece of social and cultural history. Every woman will recognise herself in the pages.'

SARAH GRISTWOOD, HISTORIAN AND AUTHOR OF *SECRET VOICES: A YEAR OF WOMEN'S DIARIES*

'Dyhouse has gifted us a clever and deeply moving exploration of family history, feminism and memory, unravelling the threads that bind our identities. Through a vivid portrayal of clothing as both expression and revelation, she reveals how garments carry our stories and connect us to our past. This book is like a family quilt, intricately woven with the textures of shared histories and personal experiences. A dazzling, evocative achievement.'

DR OWEN EMMERSON, SOCIAL AND CULTURAL HISTORIAN

'*Appearances* is Dyhouse's scrupulously researched, forensically precise, gloriously witty and personally revealing account of the importance of appearance, through the clothes, perfume, jewellery and make-up of the past and present, drawing widely from her own choices, those of her mother and daughters, and the representation of women in history, literature and the media. A brilliant cultural study that reminds us of women's "desperation of being sexy".'

PROFESSOR HELEN TAYLOR FRSA FEA, AUTHOR OF *WHY WOMEN READ FICTION*